# THE FORGOTTEN HERMITAGE OF SKELLIG MICHAEL

A CENTENNIAL BOOK

One hundred books
published between 1990 and 1995
bear this special imprint of
the University of California Press.
We have chosen each Centennial Book
as an example of the Press's finest
publishing and bookmaking traditions
as we celebrate the beginning of
our second century.

UNIVERSITY OF CALIFORNIA PRESS

*Founded in 1893*

CALIFORNIA STUDIES IN THE HISTORY OF ART

*Walter Horn, Founding Editor*
*James Marrow, General Editor*

# THE FORGOTTEN

CALIFORNIA STUDIES IN THE HISTORY OF ART, DISCOVERY SERIES II

# HERMITAGE OF SKELLIG MICHAEL

WALTER HORN

JENNY WHITE MARSHALL

GRELLAN D. ROURKE

*With Paddy O'Leary and Lee Snodgrass*

UNIVERSITY OF CALIFORNIA PRESS :: BERKELEY LOS ANGELES OXFORD

University of California Press
Berkeley and Los Angeles, California
University of California Press, Ltd.
Oxford, England

© 1990 by
The Regents of the University of California
Library of Congress Cataloging-in-
Publication Data
Horn, Walter William, 1908–
The forgotten hermitage of Skellig Michael
Walter Horn, Jenny White Marshall, and
Grellan D. Rourke with Paddy O'Leary and
Lee Snodgrass.
p.      cm.—(California studies in the history
of art. Discovery series ; 2)
ISBN 0-520-06410-0 (alk. paper)
1.  Skellig Michael (Monastery : Ireland)
2.  Christian antiquities—Ireland—Great
Skellig Island.   3.  Great Skellig Island
(Ireland)—Antiquities.   4.  Ireland—
Antiquities.   I.  Marshall, Jenny White.
II.  Rourke, Grellan D.   III.  Title.
IV.  Series.
BX2602.S54H67   1989
941.9'6—dc19                88-38692

Printed in Japan
9  8  7  6  5  4  3  2  1

The paper used in this publication meets the
minimum requirements of American
National Standard for Information
Sciences—Permanence of Paper for Printed
Library Materials, ANSI Z39.48-1984. ∞

*The publisher acknowledges*

*with gratitude the generous support*

*given this book from the Art Book Fund*

*of the Associates of the*

*University of California Press,*

*which is supported by a major gift*

*from The Ahmanson Foundation.*

# CONTENTS

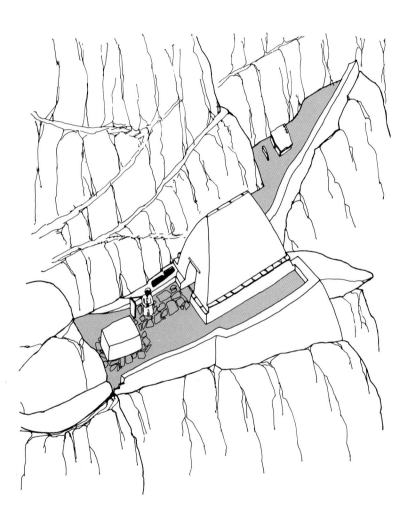

Conjectural reconstruction of the oratory terrace,
South Peak, Skellig Michael, by Grellan Rourke.

This study is not an analysis of the famous monastery of Skellig Michael, which is the subject of a separate, vastly more comprehensive, inquiry into the Early Christian architecture of Ireland in which we are involved. Instead, we wish here to guide our readers to the more treacherous peak of the island, once conquered by men who searched fearlessly for ways to reach God.

In the course of our fieldwork on Skellig Michael, we noticed architectural remains on various ledges high up on the South Peak of the island. After a thorough physical examination we could interpret these remains only as the surviving parts of an early Irish hermitage. We believe this hermitage was founded in the ninth century by a monk of the monastery of Skellig Michael, to whom even a religious settlement that accommodated no more than twelve monks and an abbot was too great a barrier between himself and God.

This investigation of the South Peak was physically our most hazardous undertaking on Skellig Michael. The peak is a conical tusk of rock whose sides slide away into the ocean with frightening steepness. Its surface is scarred by short, narrow disconnected bedrock ledges above vertical cliffs. To photograph it called first for acrobatic skills and finally for the use of aircraft, including helicopters.

Our success in studying Skellig Michael depended on the dedicated and gracious assistance of many persons. All our preliminary plans and drawings were made by Paddy O'Leary on the basis of measurements taken by him and Lee Snodgrass with the aid of a climbing rope. In the initial stages of our inquiries their part was physically the most daring. They also helped to shape both our views and the written account of our discovery.

Special mention must be made of our coauthor Grellan D. Rourke, conservation architect with the National Monuments Service, Office of Public Works, Dublin, which is in charge of site preservation on Skellig Michael. Grellan joined us later in the project, adding his invaluable expertise in architectural reconstruction and graciously contributing institutional resources. This book has been greatly enriched by his skilled observations and ideas as well as his excellent plans, drawings, and reconstructions. He and his assistants, at considerable risk, managed to survey the South Peak with a plane table, thereby providing the most accurate possible information for plans. This survey modified many of our concepts and yielded much new information.

Working with a plane table on the South Peak is so hazardous that we could write the story of the survey as an archaeological adventure. During the summer of 1986 we asked the Kerry Mountain Rescue Team how we might facilitate our dangerous reconstruction work on the monastery. Their presence on the island made possible a plane-table survey of the South Peak at the end of August 1986. Fortunately, during the nine days of the survey there was no rain, which would have made any work on the peak impossible. The weather was frequently cold, however, with winds of up to force 7 (near gale force). The site itself made progress arduous and slow, for the table had to be set up at nine different locations, sometimes in treacherous areas where there was no room to maneuver. Ropes were required as well as great concentration; a false step could have been fatal (Figs. 1 and 2). At the end, when the nine individual drawings fit neatly together, the sense of satisfaction at the accomplishment of a unique survey was enormous. It was not, however, an experience that anyone was eager to repeat.

Besides the major participants, we must give credit to other contributors who supported us in one way or another in this study. We cannot express fully our gratitude to the friend, who wishes to remain unnamed, who supported the heavy cost of photographing Skellig Michael from the air. We took most of the aerial photographs from a small Cessna, with Daphne D. C. Pochin Mould at the controls. Her knowledge of the Irish countryside from the air and her incomparable flying skill in the freakish winds on the Atlantic coast of Ireland made taking these pictures a thrilling experience.

To Frank Mitchell and Michael O'Sullivan we owe whatever we have learned about the island's geological formation. We refer to it here only summarily but shall deal with it more fully in our forthcoming book on the monastic architecture of Skellig Michael. To Des Lavelle, a descendant of two generations of lighthouse keepers and the author of a book on Skellig Michael that ought to be in the hands of anyone who is Irish, we are deeply indebted for permission to publish the photograph of the Spit with the cross slab intact. We are equally indebted to Dermot Twohig for his measurements of this upright slab.

Without the support and approval of the Commissioners of Irish Lights and the National Monuments Service of the Office of Public Works (in charge of the conservation of the island's monastery) this study could not have been undertaken. We are grateful to these agencies for their hospitality to us over many summers and to Jim Tweedy, the principal keeper of the lighthouse during this period, as well as many other lighthouse keepers who gave us counsel whenever we needed it. Michael Fitzpatrick showed us the way to the top of the peak on our first ascent. Joe Murphy and Daniel Walsh of the Office of Public Works graciously loaned us their bunkhouse on weekends, when they did not need it. We shall never forget the trust and friendship with which these men received us. Without their hospitality we could not have spent enough time on the island to study the monastery and the hermitage.

We thank that superb skipper, Dermot Walsh, who never let us down in any weather in our trips to and from the island. To him we owe our peace of mind in the midst of tumultuous seas.

Alberta Parker Horn corrected the manuscript—tedious, tiresome work that has no suitable reward. We can only acknowledge publicly our thanks and love.

In a study written collaboratively, the need for revisions and editorial corrections seems unceasing. We appreciate the unstinting attentiveness and care of our editor at the University of California Press, Stephanie Fay, in her work on this book. And we feel deeply indebted to Steve Renick, also of the Press, for his superb work in designing the book.

We are grateful to James Marrow, general editor of the California Studies in the History of Art, for having accepted this explorative work for his new Discovery Series.

We acknowledge our sources for illustrations in the captions for the various figures of this book.

Walter Horn
Jenny White Marshall

FIG. 1. *Above left:* Trying to take a measurement in a force 5 gale. John O'Brien, Aidan Forde, and Grellan Rourke working from the traverse to the outer terrace. Photograph by Dr. Michael O'Sullivan, Department of Geology, University College Cork, Ireland. Courtesy Office of Public Works.

FIG. 2. *Above:* Aidan Forde and Grellan Rourke position a ranging rod for a sighting on the outer terrace. Photograph by Dr. Michael O'Sullivan. Courtesy Office of Public Works.

# I :: THE OCCUPANCY AND ABANDONMENT OF THE ISLAND

*Delightful I think it to be in the bosom*

*of an isle, on the peak of a rock, that I*

*might often see there the calm of the sea.*

Anonymous Irish author, twelfth century

Christian monasticism had its conceptual roots in the belief that union with God could best be attained by withdrawal from civilization into harsh and isolated regions. In the third century, Egyptian Christians fled the distractions and temptations of cities to live solitary lives of prayer, meditation, and fasting in the desert. The fame of St. Anthony (ca. 251–356), the great founder of eremitic monachism, spread rapidly throughout Egypt; his duels with the devil while locked in a tomb and his decades of total isolation in the most inhospitable areas of the Egyptian desert became the heroic model for a multitude of followers.

Solitary withdrawal rapidly evolved into a form of eremitism that permitted groups of ascetics to live separately yet in proximity to one another, meeting only on Saturdays and Sundays for the celebration of a common religious service. Before Anthony died, however, another great Egyptian, St. Pachomius (292–346), introduced in southern Egypt a new concept of monastic withdrawal, one in which large groups of monks banded together to live and worship in common. Revised for the eastern Mediterranean by St. Basil of Anatolia (ca. 330–379), who became familiar with the Pachomian system while journeying in Egypt, and by St. Benedict of Nursia (ca. 480–547), who was familiar with St. Basil's concepts of monastic living, this form of collective withdrawal from the secular world became in the centuries to follow the dominant form of Christian monasticism in the lands bordering the Mediterranean and in Europe.

Yet St. Anthony's vision of solitary withdrawal into bleak areas where survival is difficult has remained over the centuries the ideal—the purest form of monastic life. From St. Simeon Stylites (ca. 390–459), who lived for decades on a pillar fifty feet high, to the nineteenth-century recluse who established himself on a volcanic plug in the Hoggar Mountains of the African Sahara, Antonian monasticism has continued to be practiced by a few highly motivated ascetics.

One of the most spectacular inaccessible regions of monastic withdrawal is in the province of Thessaly near the village of Kalabaka in Greece, where rock masses have eroded into isolated columns ranging in height from eighty-three to three hundred feet. Some have described these columns as gigantic tusks, others, as sugarloaves or gigantic stalagmites (Fig. 3). In the mid-

FIG. 3. *Above:* Meteora, Northern Thessaly, Greece. One of the dramatic geological formations near the village of Kalabaka. From the fourteenth century onward, hermits made their retreats in its cavities and recesses. Photograph by Walter Horn.

FIG. 4. *Above right:* Meteora, Northern Thessaly, Greece. The Monastery of Barlaam in the Great Meteora Complex, founded early in the sixteenth century by the brothers Nektarios and Theophanes. Drawing by C. R. Cockerell, from Donald M. Nicol, *Meteora: The Rock Monasteries of Thessaly.*

FIG. 5. *Opposite:* Skellig Michael, South Peak. A photograph of the peak from the southeast, with an arrow marking the location of the oratory terrace. Courtesy Office of Public Works, Ireland.

fourteenth century a hermit chose one of them as a place of refuge. He was soon followed by others, and eventually some of these hermitages developed into monasteries accessible only by ropes and a net worked by a windlass from above (Fig. 4). The group of monasteries is called Meteora, which means "suspended in the air."[1]

We had thought of the hermitages and monasteries of Meteora as the climax, the ne plus ultra, of monastic withdrawal until we came to work on the Irish island of Skellig Michael. In the course of investigating the island, we were startled to discover the architectural remains of a hermitage five hundred years older than the earliest hermitage of Meteora. On Skellig Michael, an island at the western edge of the European land mass—at the time the monastery was founded, the western edge of the Christian world—was a hermitage even more awesome than Meteora (Fig. 5): seven hundred feet above the sea, clinging to the narrow ledges of an austere pinnacle, the Skellig Michael hermitage is a visual wonder and a marvelous feat of construction.

1. For a general overview of Meteora see Nicol, 1963, where all previous literature is listed.

2. Frank Mitchell, written communications, 1982, 1987. Whatever we know about the time and early geological cataclysms that led to the birth of the island and its ultimate shape, we owe to the expertise and kindness of Frank Mitchell and Michael O'Sullivan, both of whom visited us on Skellig Michael on different occasions.

The island of Skellig Michael lies 11.6 kilometers off Bolus Head, the westernmost tip of the Iveragh Peninsula, County Kerry, Ireland (Map 1). The mass of rock from which the island was formed in the Devonian period some four hundred million years ago consists of hard compressed sheets of sandstone mixed with silt and gravel. During the great Armorican upheaval that created the mountains of Kerry two hundred million years later, Skellig Michael, which is connected to these mountains, rose above the sea. This mountain building was accompanied by the mass movement and translocation of rocks called jointing and faulting by geologists. Subsequent faulting and erosion over millions of years created a U-shaped depression, today named Christ's Valley or Christ's Saddle, 130 meters above sea level in the middle of the island. On either side of this small valley a peak rises, one to the northeast 185 meters high and one to the west-southwest 218 meters high (Figs. 6–8).[2]

FIG. 6. *Opposite:* Skellig Michael, aerial view from the north. Photograph by Walter Horn.

FIG. 7. *Above:* The Skellig Islands, aerial view from the west. In the foreground, the larger of the two Skelligs, Skellig Michael; in the middle ground, Little Skellig, never inhabited but used each year as a breeding ground by twenty to forty thousand gannets; in the background, the mountains of the Ring of Kerry. Photograph by Walter Horn.

MAP 1. Skellig Rocks. Location map by Grellan Rourke, 1986.

↑
N

Tralee

Dingle Peninsula

Blasket
Island

Dingle Bay

Killarney

Valentia
Island

Iveragh
Peninsula

Skellig Rocks

Beara Peninsula

Kenmare River

Bantry Bay

County
Kerry

Ireland

0  10  20  30  40  50 Km

FIG. 8. Skellig Michael, aerial view from the
south. The lower, broader summit at the northeastern end of the island became the location of
the monastery of Skellig Michael. On the high
ledges of the steeper peak at the southwestern
end are the parts of the hermitage that is the
subject of this study. The monks who came to
the island called the depression between the
peaks Christ's Saddle, a name it still retains.
Photograph by Walter Horn.

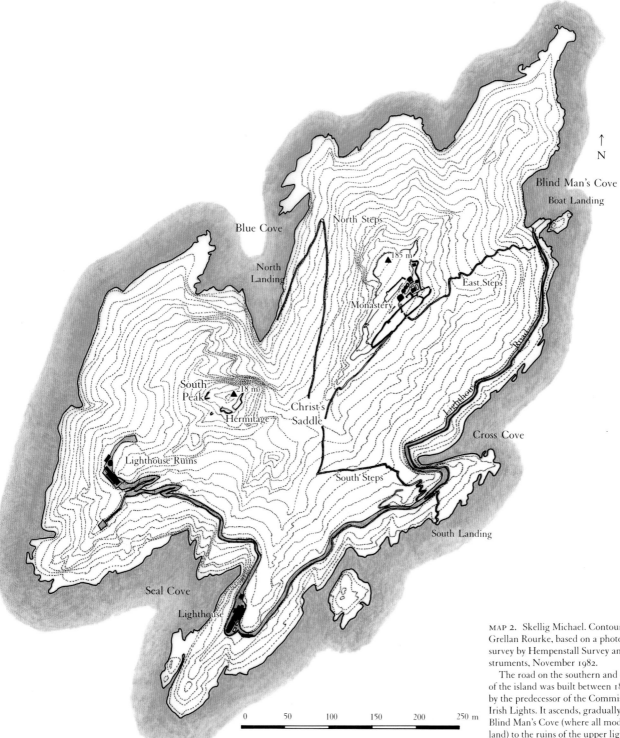

Blind Man's Cove
Boat Landing

Blue Cove

North Steps

North Landing

▲ 185 m

East Steps

Monastery

Road

South Peak

▲ 18 m

Hermitage

Christ's Saddle

Lighthouse

Cross Cove

Lighthouse Ruins

South Steps

South Landing

Seal Cove

Lighthouse

0    50    100    150    200    250 m

MAP 2. Skellig Michael. Contour map by Grellan Rourke, based on a photogrammetric survey by Hempenstall Survey and Scientific Instruments, November 1982.

The road on the southern and eastern flanks of the island was built between 1820 and 1826 by the predecessor of the Commissioners of Irish Lights. It ascends, gradually at first, from Blind Man's Cove (where all modern visitors land) to the ruins of the upper lighthouse.

The monks who founded the monastery built the stairways represented by the thinner lines on this map. The east steps, which lead to the monks' garden and then on to the oratories and beehive huts, were made inaccessible from below when the landing pier was built at Blind Man's Cove; the south steps, which start at a crude landing, ascend dramatically from Christ's Saddle toward the monastery; and the north steps, which are rarely used by modern visitors, zigzag toward Christ's Saddle, where they merge with the south steps.

Between the sixth and eighth centuries the island became a place of refuge from the world for a small settlement of ascetic monks. The broad summit on the northeastern side of the valley became the site of their monastery, comprising six beehive cells and two oratories. Probably no more than twelve monks and an abbot ever lived here at one time (Fig. 9 and Map 2).

FIG. 9. Skellig Michael. Aerial view of the monastery from the southeast (South Peak in the background). Photograph by Jim Bambury. Courtesy Office of Public Works.

3. To the best of our knowledge, this legend is first referred to in writing by Charles Smith [1756], 1969, 113.

4. *The Martyrology of Tallaght,* ed. Best and Lawlor, 1931, 37.

5. After St. Michael's appearance on Monte Gargano in Italy in 492 and on Mont-Saint-Michel in France in 708, Michael became the favorite patron saint of religious settlements located on mountains and other lofty sites. Cabrol-Leclercq, *Dictionnaire d'Archéologie et de Liturgie,* 1953, vol. 11, s.v. "Culte du Saint."

6. *Annals of the Kingdom of Ireland by the Four Masters,* ed. and trans. O'Donovan, 1851, 2: 667, 845. The entry for 1044 in the *Annals of Inisfallen,* ed. MacAirt [1951], 1977, reads simply: "Aed Sceilic, the noble priest, the celibate, and the chief of the Gaedhil in piety, rested in Christ" (209). Evidently the name Michael was still not universally used. The name Skellig Michael was used in two ninth-century entries in the *War of the Gaedhil with the Gaill* (*Cogadhh Gaedhel re Gallaibh*), written down in the early twelfth century. However, there is a strong connection between the first thirty-five chapters of this document and the *Annals of Ulster,* which is based upon a common source. "This is presumably because the compiler was using some version of the Chronicle of Ireland, the source which lies behind all the annals and which the *Annals of Ulster* preserves much more fully" (Hughes 1972, 290–95). We conclude that since no ninth-century entries in the other annals refer to the name Michael, its use in the *War of the Gaedhil with the Gaill* is due to twelfth-century scribal emendation. See also Roe (1976) for similar reasoning on the date of the use of the name Michael. We are indebted to Michael Herity for bringing this article to our attention.

Legend ascribes the founding of the monastery to St. Fionan, who lived in the sixth century.[3] The earliest documentary reference to the monastery is an entry in *The Martyrology of Tallaght,* written near the end of the eighth century by Máel-ruain (d. 792) in his monastery near present-day Dublin. It commemorates the death of a monk of Skellig called Suibni (*Suibni in Scelig*).[4] To be acknowledged in this manner in the festology of one of the most celebrated monasteries of Ireland, located at the opposite side of the country, Skellig Michael must have been a well-established and widely known monastic settlement. The monastery there may well have been founded as early as the sixth or seventh century, but in the absence of documentation more precise dating is not possible.

The monastery is referred to simply as Skellig in the eighth- and ninth-century entries in monastic festologies and annals (*The Martyrology of Tallaght,* the *Annals of Ulster,* and the *Annals of Inisfallen*). Sometime after the tenth century the monastery became known as Skellig Michael. It is likely that in the late tenth or early eleventh century the monastery was dedicated to St. Michael.[5] This is suggested by two references to the monastery in the *Annals of the Kingdom of Ireland by the Four Masters.* The first reads "Age of Christ, 950. Blathmhac of Sgeillic died"; the second, which reads "The Age of Christ, 1044. Aedh of Sgelic-Mhichil," is the first reliable mention of the name Michael in the annals.[6] On this basis we assume that the dedication to Michael took place between 950 and 1044. It was customary in a monastery to build a new church to celebrate a dedication, and the oldest part of the church now known as St. Michael's fits architecturally into this time period. With its mortared straight walls and large stones, the church is unlike the dry-stone corbeled oratories and beehive cells built earlier at the monastery.[7]

The church of St. Michael was mentioned in *The History and Topography of Ireland,* by Giraldus Cambrensis, who was in Ireland with the Normans in the late twelfth century (1183 and 1185). His account of the miraculous supply of communal wine for daily mass in St. Michael's church implies that the monastery of Skellig Michael was in constant occupancy at that time.[8]

In the thirteenth century, living conditions on the Atlantic islands of Ireland degenerated to such a degree that year-round occupancy of the island probably became impossible. A general climatic deterioration, linked to a southern shift of the circumpolar vortex, began around 1200, and as a result the polar ice cap expanded.[9] Colder weather and the increasing frequency and severity of sea storms appear to have forced the monks to withdraw to a site on the mainland on Ballinskelligs Bay, near Waterville, County Kerry.

Historical as well as climatic reasons explain why in later centuries the monastery of Skellig Michael never again came into full-time use. Many Irish monks, imitating the withdrawal of St. Anthony into the desert, sought a desert in the sea and founded monasteries on hundreds of islands—the Orkneys, the Shetlands, the Faeroes—eventually reaching from the coast of Great Britain as far as Iceland. The monastic ideal of going into exile for the love of

God, *peregrinatio pro Dei amore,* flourished in the Irish church, which was dominated by the monasteries. By the late eleventh century, however, the Irish church had begun to shift from a monastic to a diocesan structure typical of the Christian church elsewhere. At the same time, European orders of monks with no tradition of island monasticism, like the Canons Regular of St. Augustine, had established themselves in Ireland. The importance of these European monastic orders increased with the Norman conquest of Ireland in the late twelfth century. The great age of Irish eremitic island colonies, typified by Skellig Michael, was coming to an end.

The monks of Ballinskelligs monastery on Ballinskelligs Bay certainly continued to maintain and use Skellig Michael. They were proud of their association with its venerable history; in fact, in later centuries the prior of Ballinskelligs was still addressed in papal letters as "Augustinian prior of St. Michael's, Roche (*de Rupe*)." The Augustinians must have used the island intermittently, perhaps as a summer retreat. They must also have been actively involved with the pilgrims who visited the island. Skellig Michael remained in the hands of the Ballinskelligs monks until 1578, when because of the Desmond Rebellions, Queen Elizabeth I dissolved certain monasteries that were under the protection of the Earl of Desmond. At this time the island passed into private, secular, hands, where it remained until 1820, when the Corporation for Preserving and Improving the Port of Dublin, predecessor of the Commissioners of Irish Lights, purchased the island and erected two lighthouses on its Atlantic side. These were made accessible by an improved landing on the east side and a road that was blasted out on the precipitous southern flank of the island (visible in Fig. 8 and Map 2).[10]

This study describes some findings of the last few summers on the peak across the valley from the monastery. This peak, in reality the western peak of the island, has almost invariably been called the South Peak in literary references; preferring geographic to historical confusion, we will continue to use the term South Peak.

We discovered that a hermitage had been constructed on this peak during the known full-time occupancy of the island, that is, between the eighth and thirteenth centuries. One monk left the motherhouse to live as a hermit on the heights of the island's other peak.

7. Most of the ruins at the monastery belong to a later period. We will present a more detailed account of them in our forthcoming study on the monastery of Skellig Michael.

8. Giraldus Cambrensis, *Topographia Hibernica et expugnatio Hibernica,* ed. Dimock, 1867, 5: 351, translated into English under the title *The History and Topography of Ireland,* by John J. O'Meara, 1982, 80. "In the south of Munster near Cork there is a certain island which has within it a church of St. Michael, revered for its true holiness from ancient times. There is a certain stone there outside of, but almost touching, the door of the church on the right hand side. In a hollow of the upper part of this stone there is found every morning through the merits of the saints of the place as much wine as is necessary for the celebration of as many masses as there are priests to say mass on that day." Giraldus wrote from the eastern part of Ireland, never having traveled further west than Athlone in County Westmeath. This means that the monastery of Skellig Michael had a far-reaching reputation in his time.

9. This is the generally accepted theory of H. H. Lamb, 1977, 2:440–60.

10. For more information about the lighthouses, see Wilson, 1968, 53–57; and Lavelle, 1977, 54–66.

# II :: PILGRIMS AND EXPLORERS

*If the reader can conceive a person,*

*poised as it were . . . on the summit of*

*this pinnacle, beholding the vast expanse*

*of the ocean all around him . . . he may*

*be able to form some idea of the*

*tremendousness and awfulness of such*

*a prospect.*

Charles Smith, 1756

The architecture of the monastery of Skellig Michael has been the subject of a number of serious scholarly studies, the best of which were written by Liam de Paor (1955, 186) and Françoise Henry (1957, 127–29). The architectural remains on the South Peak, however, have never been acknowledged to any extent and certainly never systematically investigated.

Typically the South Peak has been written up as an exciting part of the pilgrimage to the island. For centuries Skellig Michael was famous as a place of pilgrimage and penitence. It is not known when pilgrimages to the island started, but they were flourishing in the early sixteenth century when the register of Archbishop Dowdall of Armagh mentions Skellig Michael as one of the main penitential stations in Ireland (Gogarty 1912, 1:248–76; 1913, 2:242–55). Pilgrims continued to visit Skellig Michael even after it came under the jurisdiction of the Ballinskelligs monks. Nothing is known about the monks' connection with the pilgrimages, however, nor is it known whether the sixteenth-century pilgrims sought only the monastery or the South Peak as well.

William Tirey, Bishop of Cork from 1623 to 1645, records a pilgrimage to Skellig Michael among the events of his life (Foley 1903, 16). Friar O'Sullivan, a Franciscan from Muckross who wrote the *Ancient History of the Kingdom of Kerry* about 1750, mentions in that work "the great Skelike formerly very much noted for pilgrimage over most part of Europe" (O'Sullivan 1899, 152). Soon after, in 1756, Charles Smith published the first account of the South Peak, describing the ascent of it in detail. The South Peak stations were to be visited after those of the monastery. Smith's remarks on this part of the pilgrimage suggest that a tradition of long standing was coming to an end: "Many persons about twenty years ago, came from the remotest parts of Ireland to perform these penances, but the zeal of such adventurous devotees, hath been very much cooled of late."

Smith's account of the pilgrimage to the island is concerned primarily with the dangers of the South Peak climb. For him one of the terrors of the ascent was the point where pilgrims have to squeeze through a hollow called the Needle's Eye, which resembles the funnel or shaft of a chimney. After clearing this hurdle and negotiating several other perilous passages, on each of which a stumble would mean a headlong fall, they reach the "second station . . . with utmost horror and peril." This, Smith continues ([1756] 1969, 114–15), is

> by some, called the spindle, by others the spit; which is a long, narrow fragment of the rock, projecting from the summit of this frightful place, over a raging sea; and this is walked to, by a narrow path of only two feet in breadth, and several steps in length. Here the devotees, women as well as men, get astride on this rock, and so edge forward, until they arrive at a stone cross, which some bold adventurer cut formerly, on its extreme end: and here having repeated a pater noster, returning from thence concludes [*sic*] the penance [see Figs. 43–45].

Charles Smith apparently never visited Skellig Michael. Although his description of the climb to the South Peak is reasonably accurate and is such a deliciously chilly narrative that it has been widely quoted by most later authors, his account of some of the more easily accessible parts of the island is muddled and in places completely inaccurate. For example, he locates the monastic "well" only fifty yards above the sea, although in reality the monastic water catchment cisterns lie two hundred yards above sea level within the monastic compound. In addition, he describes the ascent to the South Peak as starting directly from the grounds of the monastery, a route that would require a flight through the air across Christ's Saddle (see Fig. 8).

Succeeding accounts of the South Peak have followed Smith— both in the authors' failure to make the ascent and in the details of the descriptions. Most writers are preoccupied with the perils of the climb through the Needle's Eye, the frightening crawl out to the end of the Spit, and the dazzling view of the monastery, sea, and distant mainland from the top. Uninterested in or unaware of any archaeological remains, they have added nothing new to their accounts.[1]

Richard Hayward did climb the peak in 1946 with the aid of one of the lighthouse keepers. He was interested only in adventure and gives a dramatic description of his experiences (1946, 203–8): "Scaling several almost perpendicular sections of a precipice overhanging the sea at an altitude of more than 600 feet," he "shuffled" his way "on all fours" to the end of the Spit and there

> enjoyed all this opulent and majestic beauty clothed . . . with a strange emotional quality of remoteness and utter detachment, and I was thinking that much the same emotion might have been felt by that monk of old, who set up the little stone cross here to mark the earthbound limits of his soaring faith, limits which he had the power and grace so enduringly to transcend.

Both Smith and Hayward comment on the stone cross at the end of the Spit; neither of them, however, describes the stone accurately. Instead, both men make an intuitive assumption about its function. The stone was not

1. Writers about the South Peak who never went to Skellig Michael and/or never climbed the South Peak were Lady Chatterton, 1839, vol. 1; Stokes, 1878, 29–35; Allen, 1892, 282–84; Westropp, 1897, 308; and Foley, 1903, 16–18. Mason, 1936, 111, climbed up the South Peak but added no new information.

shaped like a cross, nor was a design engraved upon it. Nevertheless, the stone had been deliberately carried out onto the Spit, had been set in place, and was treated as a cross by the pilgrims.

The first of more systematic studies of Skellig Michael and of the South Peak began with the pioneering work of the Ordnance Survey, established in 1824. To make possible more accurate tax valuation, the maps of the Ordnance Survey delineated townland boundaries on the unprecedented scale of six inches to the mile. Moreover, the survey undertook to plot topographical features such as roads, settlements, and antiquities—in their comprehensiveness the Irish Ordnance Survey maps were unique at the time (Reeves-Smith 1983, 126).[2]

The Ordnance Survey of County Kerry, published in 1841, was directed by Thomas O'Connor. Although he did not visit the island and based his report on Smith's account, some members of his team did go to Skellig Michael and made the drawing seen in Map 3 (O'Connor 1841, 403, 405–13). It is clear that the South Peak was included in the survey of the island, for four

2. For a more detailed discussion of the making of these maps, see Andrews, 1975.

MAP 3. Ordnance Survey Map of Skellig Michael, 1841. Archives of the National Monuments Service of the Office of Public Works. Courtesy Ordnance Survey, Dublin (Archives, Ordnance Survey).

of its features are marked: "The Spit," "Stone of Pain," "Needles Eye," and, in large letters near a small rectangle, "Burial Ground." The Spit and Needle's Eye are mentioned by Smith, who also described the "Stone of Pain" with his customary bravura: "This kind of a sloping wall is about twelve feet high, and the danger of mounting it seems terrible, for if a person should slip, he might tumble on either side of the isthmus down a precipice, headlong, many fathoms into the sea" ([1756] 1969, 114, 115). Although nothing on the South Peak fits this description precisely, Smith is probably describing the last cliff face a climber ascends before arriving on the summit (see Fig. 46). When the Ordnance Survey men annotated their map with a small rectangle and the words "burial ground," however, they were the first to document the existence of possible structures on the South Peak, the first to look beyond the pilgrimage path leading up through the Needle's Eye to the Spit.

On June 23, 1851, John Windele visited Skellig Michael to study its antiquities. Windele arrived with a map that resembles a crude version of the Ordnance Survey map except for the annotations in the region of the South Peak: "Stone of Don," "Chapel," and "burial ground" (Map 4). Windele had read Smith's account of the South Peak, which contains no mention of a Stone of Don, burial ground, or chapel on the peak. Confused, therefore, he believed they were in Christ's Saddle, and he tried unsuccessfully to find them there, even asking a lighthouse keeper about them (Windele, journal entry, June 23, 1851, 7–10). Windele, who "became alarmed and nervous" climbing the steps to Christ's Saddle (Fig. 10; see also Fig. 8), had no intention of climbing the South Peak and was content to "look with shuddering interest on the fearful 'Spit' which arose at one side of it [Christ's Saddle] at an immense height nearly perpendicularly."

Why did Windele not have the official map that had been published ten years earlier, and where did he get the map he used? The Ordnance Survey map of 1841 that notes a burial ground does not include the other two annotations on Windele's map, the Stone of Don and the chapel. The Stone of Don may be the upright slab at the end of the Spit. The name Don probably derives from an incident involving Skellig that was recounted in the legendary history of the invasions of Ireland by the Milesians before the arrival of the Gael, as recorded in the *Lebor Gabála Érenn*. When the sons of Milesius were struggling with the Tuatha da Danaan for possession of Ireland, one of the two sons who died in the struggle, Don, requested burial on an island believed to be Skellig. His brother Amairgen declared that the high rock Tech Duinn, House of Donn, should be visited by the people.[3] More important, this map had the first specific mention of an oratory on the South Peak. Could Windele's map have been a rough draft made by the Ordnance Survey team who climbed the peak, one whose annotations were later changed to make them conform with Smith's description of the pilgrimage climb? Unfortunately we can find no record of such a draft.

3. *The Book of Leinster,* ed. Best, Bergin, and O'Brien, 1954, 1:1–56. See also *Lebor Gabála Érenn,* ed. and trans. Macalister, 1938–1956, pt. 1.

It was the annotations on the Ordnance Survey map of 1841 that piqued the interest of Edwin Richard Windham Wyndham-Quin, third earl of Dunraven, one of Ireland's great nineteenth-century gentlemen antiquarians, in the South Peak. Between 1866 and 1869 Lord Dunraven, accompanied by his photographer, Mercer, traveled around Ireland studying and photographing the architectural remains of ecclesiastical sites for his book *Notes on Irish Architecture.* Lord Dunraven came to Skellig Michael during this period to make the first scholarly study of the monastery for his book, still a standard in the field. While on the island he climbed the South Peak, the first

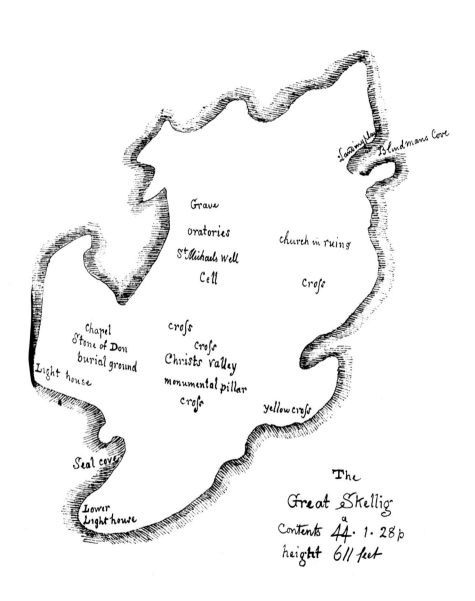

MAP 4. Map of Skellig Michael prepared by John Windele of Blair's Castle, Cork, during a visit to the island on June 23, 1851, with Edward Fitzgerald. The map is part of Windele's manuscript *Journal on Travels in Cork and Kerry, 1826–1851,* now in the Royal Irish Academy, Dublin. Courtesy Royal Irish Academy.

antiquarian to do so, and made a few brief observations vital for future investigations:

> Near the highest point of the island, which is called the Spit, I found the remains of a little building which appears to have been quadrangular, probably an oratory—all that now remains are portions of the south and west walls, with one jamb of the doorway and a cross standing near. This is probably the spot which is marked "burying place" in the map of the Ordnance Survey. There are also curious portions of an ancient wall on certain projections of rock near the Spit.
>
> (1875, 34)

Was it the presence of a cross, mentioned here for the first time, that caused Dunraven to assume that he had reached the place marked as a burial ground on the Ordnance Survey map? It is clear from his hurried, vague description that Lord Dunraven made only a quick trip to the South Peak. He took no measurements of the oratory, nor did he explore closely the "curious portions of an ancient wall on certain projections of rock near the Spit." We believe that this wall is a small section of the outer terrace visible from the route to the oratory terrace (see Figs. 44 and 51). We regret that the awkward bulk and weight of nineteenth-century cameras prevented Mercer from taking photographs.

Liam de Paor studied the monastic remains of the monastery of Skellig Michael in 1952 and 1953, and in 1955 he published his findings in a succinct but masterful description of the surviving monuments, enriched by a unique treasure of plans and sections of the entire monastery site and its individual buildings. He did not extend his study to the South Peak but did note that there were some structures on it:

> The precipitous way up to the west peak is said to have been used by pilgrims to the rock, and tradition says that the monks took refuge here during Viking raids. There are, at any rate, fairly well-defined stretches of a path winding up around the peak, and a rock-chimney ("The Eye of a Needle") which must be negotiated on the way, has hand- and foot-grips cut in it. There are faint and somewhat doubtful traces of construction at one or two points along the way, and at one place the ruined remains of a small stone structure, perched on a ledge about half-way up the peak.
>
> (1955, 186)

Françoise Henry's description of the architectural remains on the South Peak and her comments on the observations made by previous visitors

FIG. 10. Skellig Michael. View of the South Peak from the east, from the steps that ascend from Christ's Saddle to the monastery. The arrow indicates the location of the oratory terrace. Photograph by Walter Horn.

are more detailed than those of her predecessors. Unfortunately, she was unable to make the climb herself. Her emissary, however, Mr. Eugene Gillan, one of the lighthouse keepers, furnished Dr. Henry with a map of the ledge, high up on the peak, that contained the ruins of the structure identified by Lord Dunraven as an oratory (Fig. 11). Gillan's plan thus confirmed Dunraven's original observation. Dr. Henry summarizes Mr. Gillan's findings as follows:

> The plan given by Mr. Gillan corresponds with his [Lord Dunraven's] description of a rectangular building with two walls still standing. There are apparently also the traces of the two other walls, one of them projecting a little in front of the door. At the other end of the terrace are a few slabs lying flat on the ground. Mr. Gillan is of the opinion that the whole area between these and the buildings is probably paved as flags show everywhere when the loose stones which cover the platform are removed. This may be the place marked "burial ground" by the surveyors, though there is a small ledge at short distance from the terrace which has two upright slabs nearly two feet high standing side by side at a slight angle, which may also correspond to their indications.
>
> (1957, 128)

Mr. Gillan apparently had nothing to say about Lord Dunraven's additional observation of "curious portions of an ancient wall on certain projections of rock near the Spit." These remained a riddle to be solved.

None of the early or modern visitors to the island, amateur or professional, expressed the belief that the South Peak was the location of a hermitage. The romance of the pilgrim's climb, the risks involved in the ascent to the top, and the allure of the more extensive remains of the nearby monastery have diverted attention from the archaeological remains on the South Peak. Time, weather, and supply problems have also caused historians to neglect it.

FIG. 11. Skellig Michael, South Peak. The plan of the oratory terrace made for Françoise Henry by Eugene Gillan. From Henry, "Early Monasteries, Beehive Huts, and Dry-stone Houses."

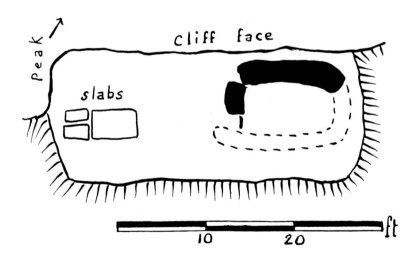

Few have ever had enough time to explore at leisure all that Skellig Michael has to offer since the normal visit to the island lasts only a few hours. A lengthy stay involves complex logistical problems because of uncertain sea and weather conditions and the lack of housing, food, and water on the island. Weather alone can wash away all resolve; very few can afford either to sit for days onshore, grimly eyeing the skies, or to huddle on the island in soggy misery awaiting those rare flashes of mercy from the Irish weather.

The observations of the Ordnance Survey of 1841, Lord Dunraven's report, the remarks of Liam de Paor, and the plan of the oratory terrace made by Eugene Gillan for Françoise Henry represented the only documentation of architectural structures when we began our own investigation in 1981.

# III :: THE ASCENT OF THE

# SOUTH PEAK

*That I might see its heavy waves over*

*the glittering ocean, as they chant a melody*

*to their Father on their eternal course.*

Anonymous Irish author, twelfth century

Our curiosity about the South Peak was aroused by Lord Dunraven's description of the ruins of an oratory on one of its highest terraces and by Gillan's plan of that terrace. For generations the South Peak had been the object of a famous pilgrimage climb; to reach the end of the Spit and there kiss the upright stone required alpine skills and cool audacity. But who had built this oratory—and for what reason? If it had been built by pilgrims or for pilgrims, why had it never been mentioned in earlier accounts of the pilgrims' climb?

We decided to find an answer to this question. For six summers, whenever the weather and a hiatus in work on the monastery of Skellig Michael permitted, we hoisted ourselves up the South Peak, laden with mountain-climbing and surveying equipment, cameras, and notebooks, to examine, measure, and record. We hope that this study stimulates a thorough archaeological examination.

For what we found—as puzzlement gave way to conjecture—appears to be the remains of one of the most daring architectural expressions of early Irish monasticism: a hermitage built virtually in the air on the treacherous ledges of an Atlantic rock rising straight up from the ocean to an altitude of 218 meters. Level surfaces on which to build the structures necessary for a hermitage did not exist. They had to be created—and were created—by the erection of walls at the brink of steeply slanting ledges, along the very boundary between life and death. These walls could have been built only by men who believed that every stone they laid brought them one step closer to God. By building a hermitage at the top of the island, they reached the ultimate goal of eremitic seclusion—a place as near to God as the physical environment would permit.

The hermitage consists of three separate terraces that we have tentatively labeled oratory terrace, garden terrace, and outer terrace. Figure 12, a reconstruction drawing, and Figure 13, an aerial view, show the topographical locations of these different terraces; the dotted line on the drawing shows the trail that connects them. The garden and oratory terraces are located near each other, on the two best natural ledges on the peak. Their spatial proximity was reinforced by the construction of two passages between them, suggesting that they had an important functional relation. The outer terrace, in contrast, is set very much apart from the oratory and garden terraces and is also the most difficult to reach.

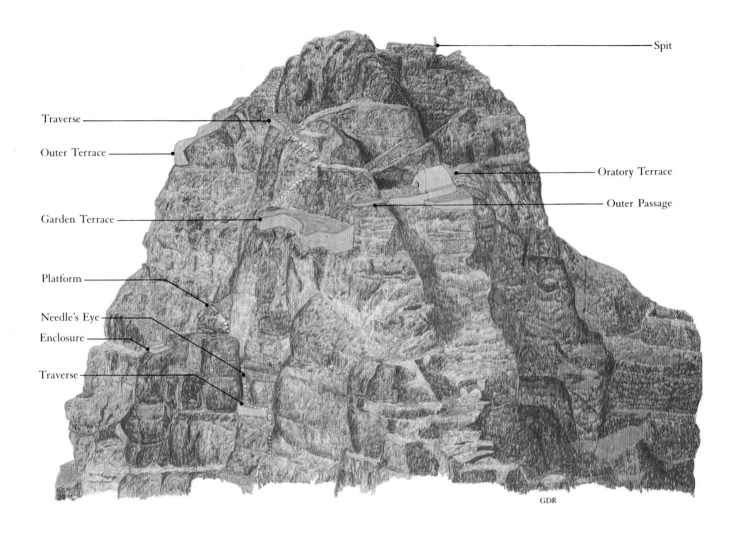

Spit

Traverse

Outer Terrace

Oratory Terrace

Outer Passage

Garden Terrace

Platform

Needle's Eye

Enclosure

Traverse

GDR

FIG. 12. Skellig Michael, South Peak. Rendering of the man-made terraces and buildings. The dotted line shows the visible portions of the route to the summit. Drawing by Grellan Rourke.

Accounts of the ascent preceding Lord Dunraven's give no reason to believe that the pilgrims of the eighteenth and nineteenth centuries knew of a hermitage on the South Peak. We can surmise that either the structures had deteriorated so as to be unrecognizable as structures or the pilgrims considered them uninteresting. Certainly by the mid-nineteenth century they must have been in poor condition, for neither the 1841 map nor Lord Dunraven's account, based on his visit in the late 1860s, connects the remnants of stone construction with the possible existence of a hermitage.

The first-time visitor, climbing the rock for penance or simply for adventure, finds the ascent itself too exacting and exciting to allow any interest in archaeological exploration. Even for our company of determined investigators, the topographical puzzle of the South Peak's religious stations began to unravel only after our fourth or fifth visit and after we had made a careful photographic survey of the peak from the air. As we became familiar with the area, we found that eighteenth- and nineteenth-century accounts had exag-

FIG. 13. Skellig Michael, South Peak. Aerial view of the peak from the south, showing (near bottom left) the Needle's Eye, (above it to the right) the garden terrace and the oratory terrace on their respective levels, and (to the left of the other terraces) the wall of the outer terrace. Photograph by Walter Horn. (See Fig. 8 for a view of the entire island from the south.)

gerated the dangers of the climb. Wherever possible, the builders of the trail to the top of the peak had aided the ascent by constructing dry-stone traverses and masonry steps or, in the steeper places where such construction was not possible, by cutting toeholds and handgrips in the rock face.

But only a climber with a good head for heights and reasonable physical agility should ever try the ascent, and no one should attempt it when the ground is wet or when gusting winds lash the island. In the more precipitous passages the danger is immediately visible, but elsewhere the hazards are less obvious. In several places along the trail, the ledges were improved with masonry additions, and massive masonry bridges were constructed across impassable gullies. Now after a thousand years, however, much of this masonry work is slipping away (see, for example, the masonry traverse leading to the Needle's Eye, visible in Fig. 18, where the badly subsided masonry is unpredictable and must be approached with extreme caution).

FIG. 14. *Right:* Skellig Michael. Christ's Saddle, western slope. The footpath leads to the starting point of the trail to the Needle's Eye. Figure 10 shows this same slope from a perspective that includes the South Peak (note the rocks at center right here, also visible at lower left in Fig. 10). The steps in the foreground climb from Christ's Saddle to the monastery (Map 2 shows the location of the island's stairways). Near the lower part of the trail to the South Peak is a cavelike shelter (arrow) that may have been used as a penitential retreat or temporary hermitage by the Skellig monks. A cross is engraved on the rock at the entry to the shelter. Photograph by Walter Horn.

FIG. 15. *Opposite:* Skellig Michael, South Peak. Natural ledge of rock curving around the South Peak to the Needle's Eye (dotted line marks the path). Photograph by Walter Horn.

FROM CHRIST'S SADDLE TO THE NEEDLE'S EYE

From the lowest point of Christ's Saddle a green slope rises to the narrow ridge connecting the South Peak with a massive outcropping of rocks to the south (Fig. 14). At the northern end of that ridge, at its very juncture with the South Peak, the ascent to the summit begins. A short, steep cleft containing remains of masonry steps leads to a natural ledge that spirals around the western face of the peak (Fig. 15).

FIG. 16. *Above:* Skellig Michael, South Peak. Steps cut into the rock ledge on the path to the Needle's Eye. Photograph by Walter Horn.

FIG. 17. *Right:* Skellig Michael, South Peak. Blind corner (at the top of the steps) in the path to the Needle's Eye. Note the crag at left, which is visible in Figure 8 as a point of rock to the left of and below the summit. Photograph by Walter Horn.

FIG. 18. *Opposite:* Skellig Michael, South Peak. The Needle's Eye. Its entrance is reached by a short traverse of dry-stone masonry at the top of a steep rock face. The masonry has deteriorated, bulging and subsiding dangerously. Photograph by Walter Horn.

Initially, passage is comfortable and easy along the broad trail (Fig. 16). After some forty meters, however, the ledge becomes steep, narrows to half a meter, and turns a blind corner (Fig. 17). Notwithstanding the steps cut into the rock face at the turn, no one with vertigo would attempt to negotiate this intimidating corner, where the drop-off is seventy meters. From the path one can see an awesome natural formation on an adjacent crag that one is tempted to interpret as a station of the cross. After the blind corner, the path

levels out once more and broadens before ending at the foot of a massive rock. At the top of this rock is the formation that has become famous in the legend of the South Peak: the Needle's Eye.

The Needle's Eye (Fig. 18), the gate to the upper part of the peak, is a narrow rock chimney formed by a vertical crack in the massive block projecting horizontally from the principal body of the peak. The entrance to the chimney, some five meters above the path, is reached by climbing a rock face on which steps have been cut deeply enough to serve as toeholds, none of which, however, accommodates an entire foot. A dry-stone traverse about four meters long and one meter wide was built to provide level access to the base of the Needle's Eye.[1] Beautifully constructed and vital for a safe passage, it is now untrustworthy.

   The ascent through the high narrow shaft of the Needle's Eye is aided by well-defined natural spurs and fissures as well as by chiseled grips for feet and fingers on the side walls and on a central rock running up the chim-

1. The depth of the fill on the traverse varies from .70 meter to 2 meters. Eight masonry steps, each .64 meter wide and curving slightly to the left, were built into the traverse at the southwest end to permit access from the rock face to the top of the traverse. Construction of this rather wide, level access may have been necessary to facilitate transportation and temporary storage of building materials and supplies here.

FIG. 19. *Above:* Skellig Michael, South Peak. Entry to the Needle's Eye. Footholds are cut into a vertical rock in the center of the chimney. The chimney itself varies in width from half a meter to a meter. Photograph by Walter Horn.

FIG. 20. *Above right:* Skellig Michael, South Peak. The Needle's Eye. View down the shaft from the last of the four steps cut into the inner wall of the chimney above the spine of rock shown in Figure 19. Photograph by Walter Horn.

## FROM THE NEEDLE'S EYE TO THE HERMIT'S GARDEN

2. After negotiating the chimney, the climber steps onto the lower of these platforms (not visible in photographs), which extends almost 4 meters. Up three rock-cut steps is the second platform, which runs for 7 meters, ending abruptly at a rock face. Another possible reason for their construction may have been the need for access to areas for bird hunting on the north side of the peak.

ney (Fig. 19). Climbers must hoist themselves up seven meters, alternately lifting the body and then bracing it against the chimney walls while searching for the next support. Without these supports, climbers would require acrobatic skills to inch up the shaft. Even now it is not easy because the distance from the first to the second step is over a meter. The passage is especially difficult on the downward journey.

Climbing is easier near the top of the chimney where the central rock develops into well-defined steps (Fig. 20). The climber stepping out of the Needle's Eye discovers the first of several perplexing structures on the South Peak. Two crescent-shaped masonry platforms (see Fig. 57) were built here, one slightly higher than the other, that have no connection with the climb to the top. Possibly the monks used them as construction platforms, level areas on which to pile building materials brought up the chimney by rope.[2]

The remains of another odd structure lie nearby, separated from the trail leading to the top and visible only from above. On the far side of the Needle's Eye are the remains of a small U-shaped enclosure built on a level spur facing west to the sea (Fig. 21). Access is awkward, requiring a scramble up and over the large rock that is the west side of the Needle's Eye. This time no helpful handholds or toeholds mark the way.

FIG. 21. Skellig Michael, South Peak. The rectangular masonry enclosure (upper arrow) at
the outer edge of the Needle's Eye. The exit
from the Needle's Eye is at the lower arrow, and
in the background, at left, are the ruins of the
Upper Lighthouse. Photograph by
Walter Horn.

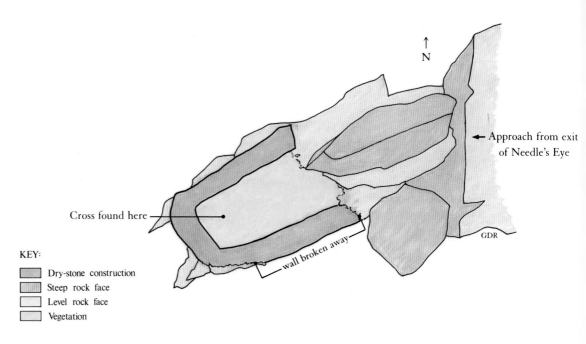

Cross found here

KEY:

Dry-stone construction
Steep rock face
Level rock face
Vegetation

wall broken away

N

GDR

FIG. 22. *Above:* Skellig Michael, South Peak. Drawing by Grellan Rourke of the small enclosure near the Needle's Eye, based on the 1986 survey of the hermitage by Grellan Rourke and Richard Stapleton.

FIG. 23. *Below:* Skellig Michael, South Peak. Fragment of a cross found in the small enclosure. Drawing by Grellan Rourke.

Present condition         Reconstruction

worked                    GDR

0    5    10   15   20   25 cm

3. The cleft has been artificially widened; at least .5 square meter was removed (presumably by the monks) from the western, entrance, side to facilitate access to the terrace (O'Sullivan 1987).

The inside of the enclosure is about 2.3 meters long and 1.2 meters wide; the wall varies in thickness from .35 to .50 meter (Fig. 22). Although the enclosure wall now is rather low, with stone rubble filling the interior, it is still possible to trace both the inside and the outside except at the entry and externally at the southwestern corner, where it has fallen away. The masonry, of fairly small-sized stones, is difficult to judge, but the scale and technique of construction are those of a rectilinear enclosure wall, not those of the base of a cell. Judging from the amount of fallen stone and taking into consideration stone that has fallen over the edge, we calculate that the original wall may have been from 1 meter to 1.5 meters high.

A short length of wax candle and a fragment of a rude stone cross, identical to crosses in the monastery graveyard, lay under collapsed stone in the enclosure (Fig. 23). Was this a place for a hermit to pray and meditate?

After the detour to the enclosure, the climber returns to the trail above the Needle's Eye and continues to ascend, making a sharp turn to the right. The next task is scaling a rough-textured rock gully nearly fifteen meters high (see Figs. 12, 13). Here again progress is aided by toeholds, although these are not always easy to recognize because plants, also seeking a foothold on the irregular surface, fill the crevices of the gully.

At the top of the gully the climber finds, in a narrow rock cleft (Fig. 24), masonry steps that lead to the first and lowest of the three hermitage stations, one that has never before been recognized and is nowhere mentioned in the accounts of previous visitors to the site (Fig. 25).[3] The reason for this omission is simple: the climber stepping onto this terrace with surprise and relief cannot see that it has been constructed. The walls holding the terrace in place, invisible to anyone ascending the gully to the terrace or standing on it, can be seen only if one leans far over the edge, something few visitors would think of doing.

FIG. 24. *Left:* Skellig Michael, South Peak. The garden terrace from above. The narrow rock cleft that provides access to the terrace is at the lower right. Paddy O'Leary (top), secured by a rope held by Lee Snodgrass, examines the retaining wall. Photograph by Walter Horn.

FIG. 25. *Below:* Skellig Michael, South Peak. Aerial view of the garden terrace. Photograph taken in 1987 by Con Brogan. Courtesy Office of Public Works. Dotted lines indicate the two passages to the oratory terrace, the upper one over the hump of rock that separates the two terraces, the lower one around its outer face.

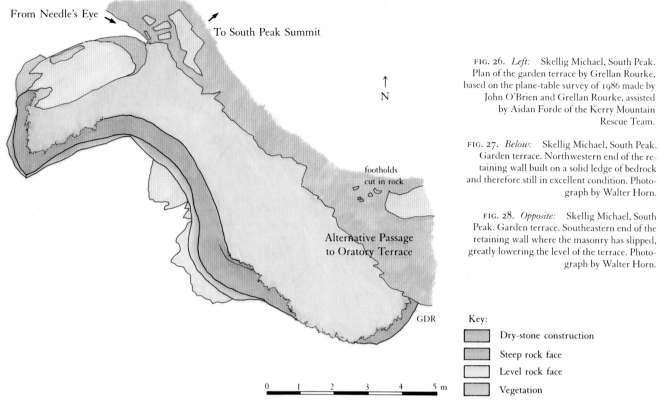

From Needle's Eye

To South Peak Summit

↑
N

footholds
cut in rock

Alternative Passage
to Oratory Terrace

GDR

Key:

Dry-stone construction

Steep rock face

Level rock face

Vegetation

0   1   2   3   4   5 m

FIG. 26. *Left:* Skellig Michael, South Peak. Plan of the garden terrace by Grellan Rourke, based on the plane-table survey of 1986 made by John O'Brien and Grellan Rourke, assisted by Aidan Forde of the Kerry Mountain Rescue Team.

FIG. 27. *Below:* Skellig Michael, South Peak. Garden terrace. Northwestern end of the retaining wall built on a solid ledge of bedrock and therefore still in excellent condition. Photograph by Walter Horn.

FIG. 28. *Opposite:* Skellig Michael, South Peak. Garden terrace. Southeastern end of the retaining wall where the masonry has slipped, greatly lowering the level of the terrace. Photograph by Walter Horn.

During our first two visits we too were unaware that we were standing on a man-made terrace. On our third visit, we leaned over the edge and took the photographs shown in Figures 27 and 28. In 1982, Paddy O'Leary and Lee Snodgrass measured the platform; later, in 1986, Grellan Rourke made the plan shown in Figure 26.

The kidney-shaped terrace is thirteen meters long and varies in width from two to four meters. The long axis of the terrace runs roughly from northwest to southeast. The retaining wall, 1.5 meters high at the northwestern end of the platform, is built on firm bedrock (Fig. 27). This section of the wall is in impeccable condition, as solid as when first constructed. It is identical in style with the best dry-stone masonry found in the monastery itself (see Fig. 33). Toward the southeastern end of the platform the height of the retaining wall decreases in places to as little as .3 meter (Fig. 28). Here the courses are no longer horizontal but jumbled, an effect characteristic of subsidence, doubtless caused by their construction on the section of the ledge that tilts briskly southeastward. At present there is a drop of 2.4 meters between the northwestern and the southeastern ends of the terrace; estimates based on

4. Rourke estimates that such a wall could have retained approximately 45 cubic meters of fill; 14 cubic meters have fallen away, so that only about 31 cubic meters are now being retained. Michael O'Sullivan (1987) cautions that the distribution of the underlying bedrock is unknown, and therefore these figures must be considered maximal, for they assume that the bedrock profile is relatively planar.

5. This is the opinion of O'Sullivan (1987), who notes in addition the possibility that the sandstone cobbles on the terrace, much smaller than those found in Skellig coves, may have been brought from the mainland.

6. *Vitae Sanctorum Hiberniae,* ed. Plummer, 1910, 2:13.

7. There is no literary evidence to attest that sea birds were an integral part of the diet of the monks of Skellig Michael, but Michael O'Kelly, excavating nearby Church Island, found that the monastic inhabitants had eaten gannet, shag, cormorant, white-fronted goose, and duck (O'Kelly 1958, 130). Bird eating is common among secular inhabitants of the Atlantic islands. For the old St. Kildan tradition of eating birds and birds' eggs, see Martin, *A Voyage to St. Kilda,* 1698; Macaulay, *The Story of St. Kilda,* 1764; Maclean, *Island on the Edge of the World,* 1980. For a general discussion of the birds that breed on the Skellig rocks, see Des Lavelle, 1977, 68–83.

this drop suggest that at least 40 percent of the original terrace fill is no longer there. The southeastern section of the wall, now only .3 meter high, would have needed to be approximately 3 meters high to create a level terrace.[4] The original terrace wall was probably never more than a meter above the present level of the northwestern section, as the walls are too thin and roughly constructed on the inner face to have supported a greater height.

Although we call this platform the garden terrace, its function is open to speculation. A masonry traverse or passage was not needed for the climb to higher terraces or to the summit. In fact, the path continues upward just at the point of access to the terrace in an unbroken line of solid rock (see the upper passage indicated on Fig. 25). Furthermore, there are no definite remains or other visible evidence that any structures were ever built on this platform. There is, therefore, no immediately apparent reason for its creation. The possibility that it was built to provide space for a garden warrants further discussion.

The lowest platform is by far the best place on the South Peak for a garden. Its northwest-to-southeast axis gives it full exposure to sunlight from late morning to evening. At the northwestern end of the terrace the wall is only about half a meter wide, with a ragged inner face composed of stones smaller than those on its smooth outer face—an indication that the inner face was never meant to be seen, at least at this level. Moreover, the soil on this terrace, unlike the typically heavy, wet soil of the South Peak, is light and dry, thus ensuring good drainage. Scattered throughout the soil are thousands of small sharply faceted stones that are clearly detritus, fragments of quarried rock. Much of this stone fill is from rocks not indigenous to the South Peak. In addition, there are some sandstone cobbles that may have come from Seal Cove or Cross Cove (see Map 2).[5] Clearly, a considerable amount of the fill for this terrace was brought up the peak. Neither here nor in the monastery gardens is there evidence of an irrigation system; evidently rainfall provided sufficient moisture to raise plants in this climate.

Because agricultural work was a necessary part of a monk's responsibility, important for the health of both body and soul, gardens were an integral part of monastic life. Vegetables, furthermore, are often mentioned in the literature as an essential part of the monastic diet. Some austere diets, like that of the Bangor monks under the rule of Abbot Comgall, consisted of vegetables supplemented with bread.[6] The diet of island monks, however, differed somewhat from that of mainland monks. The staples of Irish monks living on the North Atlantic islands from Ireland to Iceland were, of necessity, fish and the meat and eggs of the birds nesting on these islands.[7] Grain for bread was not easily obtainable, as it required more growing space than most islands possessed. Therefore vegetables were particularly important as a dietary supplement. Striking evidence of the importance of monastic gardens can be seen in the extensive terraces that served as gardens for the monastery of Skellig Michael (see Fig. 9).

A garden, moreover, would have spiritual importance to a hermit because it would help him to maintain his solitude and independence from the

FIG. 29. Skellig Michael, South Peak. Oratory terrace. Aerial view from the southeast, showing the surviving walls of the oratory and, on the collapsed outer section of the terrace, the remaining masonry fragments of the retaining wall. Dotted lines mark the two approaches to the oratory terrace from the garden terrace, the upper one over the hump of rock between them, the lower one around its outer edge. Photograph by Walter Horn.

monastery. In the seventh century St. Cuthbert, abbot of Lindisfarne, retired to Farne Island to live a life of eremitical solitude. The tiny island, with no water, no food, and no trees, was perfect for an ascetic monk. St. Cuthbert's monks helped him to establish his hermitage, building an enclosure wall, carving a well out of rock, and constructing "such essential buildings as an oratory and a communal shelter [that is, one for domestic use]." St. Cuthbert then ordered his monks to bring him gardening utensils and seed, for he intended to live an independent life: "If God's grace will enable me to live in this place by the labour of my own hands, I shall gladly remain there; but if it proves otherwise, then, God willing, I will soon return to you."[8]

8. Bede, *A History of the English Church and People,* trans. Sherley-Price, 1955, 261–62. For the Latin see *Two Lives of St. Cuthbert,* ed. and trans. Colgrave, 1940. As late as 1084 the charters of Kells mention a permanent *disert,* "hermitage," with a garden for wandering hermits: "These [charters of Kells] have all granted for ever Disert-Columcille in Kells, with its vegetable garden, to God and *devout pilgrims,* no wanderer having any lawful possession in it at any time until he surrender his life to God, and is devout" (Adamnan, 1874, cxxv; italics in original).

The second and most important of the three eremitic stations of the South Peak, the oratory terrace, lies at right angles to the garden terrace four meters above it, with a rock barrier separating the two terraces both physically and visually. There are two ways to travel from the garden to the oratory terrace. The most obvious and safest way is to continue the climb to the summit from the northwestern end of the terrace, on a series of steps cut into the rock. The steps lead to the top of the long rock ridge separating the garden and oratory terraces. At the top of the ridge a left turn (to the northwest) leads to the final ascent to the summit, and a right turn leads down to the oratory terrace (Fig. 29).

FROM THE GARDEN TERRACE
TO THE ORATORY TERRACE

FIG. 30. Skellig Michael, South Peak. Oratory terrace, looking east, before the clearing of the sea campion. At left, the surviving parts of the north and west walls of the oratory; beyond the terrace, the slanting surface of the monastery summit of Skellig Michael. Only the domes of two beehive huts and an oratory are visible from this angle. Little Skellig and the mountains of the Ring of Kerry are visible beyond the monastery. Photograph by Jenny White Marshall.

9. The outer passage varies in width between .6 meter and 1.5 meters.

Originally another connection led from the southeastern end of the garden to the oratory terrace, up steps that are now barely discernible in the rock face and along the outer edge of the ridge between the two terraces. The existence of this outer passage is further evidenced by the dry-stone masonry buttressing a large slab on this ledge.[9] Fragments of the masonry can be seen only from the air or through binoculars from lower levels of the island (see Fig. 25). At the far end of the ledge, precipitous steps cut into the ridge led down to the retaining wall of the oratory terrace (at the end of the outer passage shown in Fig. 29). The passage, a shortcut between the two terraces, is dangerous in windy or wet weather, particularly at the narrow juncture with the oratory terrace, where the retaining wall no longer exists. Because of the danger of this juncture, we conclude that the passage was built after the construction of the retaining wall for the oratory terrace.

FIG. 31. Skellig Michael, South Peak. Oratory
terrace, with the west wall of the oratory freed
from its overgrowth of sea campion, revealing
a flagged path and steps descending to the
water basins on the north side of the oratory.
Photograph by Jenny White Marshall.

This station, lying about two hundred meters above the ocean and some fifteen meters below the summit, offers a magnificent view of the seascape east
of the island (Figs. 30, 31). Until we cleared away the sea campion, it flourished, almost covering the remains of two walls of the oratory. Beyond the
terrace, on the other side of Christ's Saddle, the domes of the monastery's
beehive cells are seen on the northeastern summit, with the dramatic sil-
houette of Little Skellig rising behind. In the background, the delicate curve
of the mountains of the Iveragh Peninsula, more than eleven kilometers to the
east, frames the seascape.

   Over time, the oratory terrace has suffered so severely from the
collapse of its retaining walls that it is perilous to examine, and its original

form is hard to establish. O'Leary and Snodgrass, belayed by ropes, surveyed the site with plumb lines in the summer of 1982. In 1986, Rourke resurveyed the South Peak with a plane table, and on the basis of that survey he drew the plan shown in Figure 32. The surviving remains, according to his findings, are

1.  The north wall and much of the entrance wall of an oratory.
2.  Two interconnecting water basins located at the base of a flagged path at the northwestern corner of the oratory.
3.  Flagstones under fallen masonry at the entrance to and in front of the oratory, believed to be the remains of a completely paved terrace.
4.  A rectangular *leacht,* a low dry-stone structure shaped like an altar, at the place where Eugene Gillan's plan (see Fig. 11) shows three objects labeled slabs. Hidden from sight by a dense overgrowth of sea campion, this structure is probably what the Ordnance Survey plan of 1841 identified as a burial ground.
5.  Midway between the oratory and the *leacht,* lying flat on its back, a cross inscribed on a slab that, like the *leacht,* was hidden from sight by sea campion. This is most likely the standing cross mentioned by Lord Dunraven in 1875.
6.  A small extension of the terrace east of the oratory that contains two stone slabs placed on edge at right angles to each other (Eugene Gillan mentioned them but did not show them on his plan) and a third upright slab, or orthostat, hidden by sea campion, slightly behind the other two.
7.  Fragments of masonry that once formed part of a retaining wall around the perimeter of the oratory terrace.

Many of these features, with the exception of the slab incised with a cross and the paving slabs, are visible in aerial photographs like that of Figure 29. They are described in the following pages.

The Oratory

10. Plinths on the east and south sides at a slightly higher level than the one on the western side are conjectured for two reasons: tradition and the knowledge that this arrangement increases the strength of a structure that has no plinth on the north side but a path 1.18 meters above the pavement level.

The remains of this structure consist of much of the north wall and adjoining west wall. The north wall is the more intact because it was built on bedrock as close to the rock face as possible. Its maximum height is 1.35 meters above the level of the threshold. Corbeling is evident. The internal length of the remaining north wall is 2.55 meters; the internal width of the oratory wall is 2.1 meters, with a narrow entry (.57 meter) midway in the wall. Precise overall dimensions are difficult to determine owing to collapse, but when the proportions of the small oratory in the monastery are related to this structure, they yield an estimated length of 2.75 meters. On the western, entry, side there is a plinth approximately .36 meter above the level of the threshold.[10]

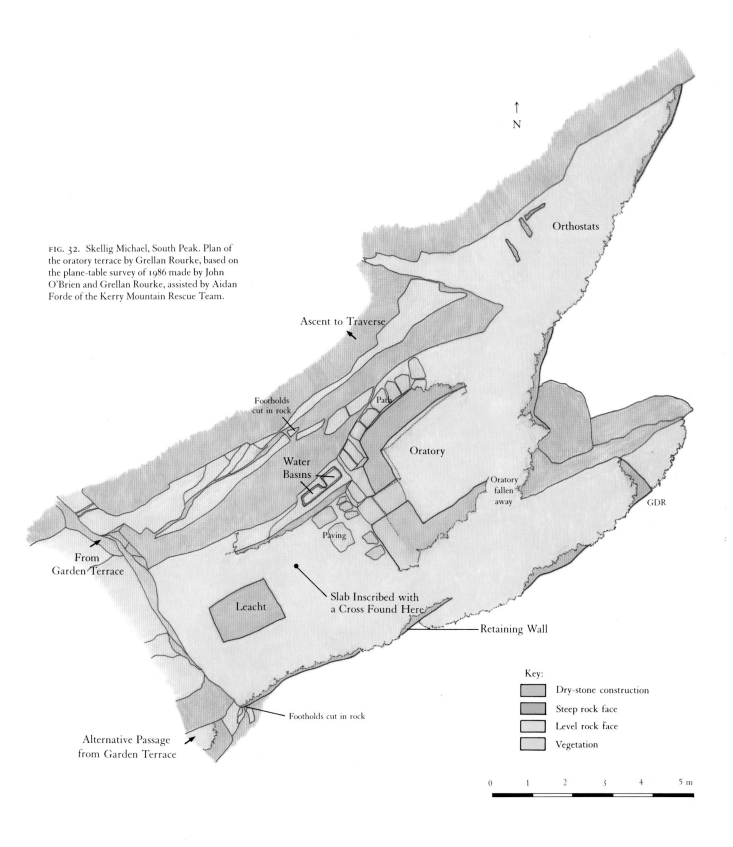

FIG. 32. Skellig Michael, South Peak. Plan of the oratory terrace by Grellan Rourke, based on the plane-table survey of 1986 made by John O'Brien and Grellan Rourke, assisted by Aidan Forde of the Kerry Mountain Rescue Team.

↑
N

Orthostats

Ascent to Traverse

Footholds
cut in rock

Path

Oratory

Water
Basins

Oratory
fallen
away

GDR

Paving

From
Garden Terrace

Leacht

Slab Inscribed with
a Cross Found Here

Retaining Wall

Key:

Dry-stone construction

Steep rock face

Level rock face

Vegetation

Footholds cut in rock

Alternative Passage
from Garden Terrace

0    1    2    3    4    5 m

11. Other well-preserved examples illustrating this distinction between the designs of oratories and dwellings exist at the monasteries of Inishmurray and Illauntannig, both built, like Skellig Michael, on treeless islands. For further discussion of the distinction between circular dwellings and rectangular oratories see Horn, 1973, 23–31.
12. On the adoption of architectural features peculiar to timber construction in Irish stone churches see Leask, 1955, vol. 1, chaps. 5 and 6. His theory has been generally accepted (Thomas, *Early Christian Archaeology,* 1971, 75; and de Paor and de Paor [1958], 1967, 58–60).

These fragments of wall indicate a rectangular structure aligned east to west and built of dry-stone masonry. Of the buildings in a monastery of the Early Christian period, only an oratory fits this description. All oratories—and oratories alone—were rectangular structures with longitudinal axes running east to west. The monks of this period, by contrast, dwelt in circular houses, a custom inherited from their secular ancestors. A typical example of this architectural distinction is seen in the layout of the monastery that the monks of Skellig Michael built on the other side of Christ's Saddle. It comprises six circular beehive cells and two rectangular oratories, the larger one measuring 2.44 by 3.67 meters inside, the smaller one 1.83 by 2.44 meters.[11]

The dry-stone architecture of the hermit's oratory is typical of Early Christian oratories commonly found on the islands off the west coast of Ireland, where timber was unavailable. In part, their design translated into stone the curved walls and roofs of the cruck-built timber churches that abounded during this period on the mainland of Ireland, where timber was easily obtainable.[12]

The masonry technique of the hermit's oratory, as exemplified in the remains of the north and west walls, is identical with that of the two oratories in the monastery. The smaller of the two is illustrated in Figure 33. All oratories built in this style have very thick corbeled walls with stones laid horizontally; none use mortar, dressed stones, or a rigid system of coursing. The walls in these structures were built of well-chosen medium-sized stones filled in with small stones to produce a well-compacted, even surface.

### The *Leacht*

At the western end of the terrace approximately one meter east of the rock face are the remains of a rectangular stone-built structure 1.1 by 1.6 meters; its present height above the level of the pavement is .45 meter (Fig. 34). The basic structure is well preserved, but the uppermost level has been damaged by weathering. This setting of stones is the remains of a *leacht.*

*Leachta,* square or rectangular structures built of rough, unmortared stones, are associated with Irish Early Christian monastic sites. Today they are found primarily at the island monasteries off the west coast of Ireland. Their original distribution is unknown, as they are easily destroyed, but because some have been found in northern Britain, we know they were not limited to the western coastline. Outstanding examples are found today in the monasteries of Skellig Michael, Illauntannig, and Inishmurray. A typical example of a *leacht* from Inishmurray is shown in Figure 35. It is a quadrangular mass of masonry roughly one meter high, with a tall engraved cross slab set in its center (Wakeman 1893, 71, Fig. 34).

13. Thomas, in *Early Christian Archaeology,* 1971, 169–75, gives the best summary of our current state of knowledge.

The function of *leachta* has long been debated. They may have been used to mark burial places, particularly for special saints, or to house relics, mostly the bones of saints; or they may have served as places for prayer, either as stations of the cross or as altars for celebrating mass. It is quite possible that all of these conjectures are correct and that *leachta* served different functions in different times and places.[13] Only the systematic excavation of a carefully selected group of Irish *leachta* might ascertain their precise function.

FIG. 33. *Above:* Monastery of Skellig Michael. View from the south of the small oratory that served as the model for Grellan Rourke's reconstruction in Figure 39. Photograph by Walter Horn.

FIG. 34. *Left:* Skellig Michael, South Peak. Remains of a *leacht*. Photograph by Walter Horn.

FIG. 35. *Above:* Island monastery of Inishmurray, County Sligo. A *leacht,* referred to
locally as *altóir beag,* "the little altar," one of
approximately fifteen *leachta* on Inishmurray
of similar construction. Three lay within the
monastery's walls; twelve along the periphery
of the island served as pilgrimage stations.
Photograph by Walter Horn.

FIG. 36. *Right:* Skellig Michael, South Peak.
Oratory terrace. The cross slab discovered in
1982 at the location indicated in the plan of the
terrace (Fig. 32). Photograph by Lee Snodgrass.

Some *leachta,* however, are known to contain human bones. The larger of the two *leachta* in the Skellig Michael monastery is situated north of the large oratory; the other, smaller, one is built against the monastery retaining wall south of the large oratory. In the course of badly needed repair to the perimeter of these *leachta,* the National Monuments Service found some human bones. Because the bones were discovered by chance during the rebuilding of the wall face, not in the course of an excavation, no attempt was made to explore the *leachta* in depth, and the bones were returned to their original position.

The remains of a *leacht* on the South Peak oratory terrace give evidence of a structure too small to be the original burial place of anyone. Possibly this *leacht* was either a memorial shrine, containing the translated bones of a hermit, or an altar.

While taking measurements on the oratory platform, Snodgrass noticed the unusual shape of the top of a rabbit burrow. Carefully pulling aside a few tufts of sea campion, she discovered a smooth thin slab of slate with a ring cross engraved on it (Fig. 36). This is almost certainly the cross slab Lord Dunraven described in 1875 as "standing near" the oratory (see p. 18). It is a fortunate discovery because the design of the cross furnishes a clue to the date of the hermitage. Unfortunately, the slab is broken, and much of the upper part of the ring-cross design is missing. The missing fragment was not in any place accessible to surface inspection and would be difficult to find without excavation unless rabbits in the future decide to burrow in strategic places. The cross slab was placed in the care of the National Monuments Service.[14]

Such a cross slab located in the open space in front or to the side of an oratory is a classic feature of early Irish hermitages and monasteries, as Michael Herity has shown in a recent study (1984, 105–16). The chronological implications of the design on the slab are discussed in the Appendix.

The Stone Slab Fragment Inscribed with a Cross

14. O'Sullivan (1987) believes that this slate slab may have been brought to the island.

To gain access to the oratory terrace, one follows a natural ledge with steps cut into it that zigzags down the face of the cliff to a flagged path below. The existence of this path was unknown until Rourke removed sea campion from around the north wall of the oratory. At the western end of the path, steps lead down to the oratory; at the foot of these steps a critical feature turned up: two interconnecting basins chiseled out of the rock (Fig. 37). Their shape and location clearly indicate that they were used for collecting water.

This dramatic discovery gave us tangible proof of our hypothesis that a hermit lived on the South Peak. Anchorites tended to reduce their dietary needs to the lowest margin, but water was an indispensable daily requirement. The purpose for planning and constructing sophisticated water basins could only have been to enable someone to inhabit this barren crag.

On the cliff face north of the oratory two man-made grooves direct water into the basins. Water was also collected and fed into them by a channel cut under the flagstone path, visible near its termination at the base of the steps. When the water reached a certain height in the first basin, it overflowed

The Water-Collecting Basins

into the second, slightly bigger, basin. This arrangement permitted the cleaning of one basin while water was retained in the second and also helped filter the water. Another component of this clever filtering system is the circular depression that collected silt at the feed end of the first basin. Careful consideration had been given to long-term use of these basins. They were near the oratory simply because there, coincidentally, the large fractured surface of the rock wall provided the best source of water.

This whole area was meticulously planned. That the masonry of the north oratory wall was built over the channel that directed water into the basins shows that the basins were carved prior to the construction of the oratory. Moreover, the northwestern corner of the oratory near the bottom of the steps is notched so that someone descending the steps has a space to turn and can avoid stepping into the water basins.

Water is always in short supply on Skellig Michael, which possesses no natural springs or wells, and must be collected from the rain that trickles down sloping rock surfaces into man-made cisterns. The vast inclined surface of rock rising behind the monastery was the source of water for the monastic community. The monks constructed two large cisterns to collect and store water running off this surface. The shortage of water on Skellig Michael and the logistics of carrying it from the monastery across Christ's Saddle and up the South Peak are practical reasons for a hermit to have established his own water supply. An equally important spiritual reason would be the desire to maintain solitude and independence from the monastery—the same desire that prompted hermits to establish gardens.

In its original form the oratory terrace consisted of two parts: the principal area, accommodating the features just discussed, and an extension toward the east. The present length of the oratory terrace, including its eastern extension, is eighteen meters. Its greatest width is 6.7 meters. Access to the eastern extension today is dangerous; sea campion hides whatever is left of the wall that once supported a level and secure passage. There are hints of a stone wall along the outer edge of the terrace, but this area has collapsed so severely and the drop is so sheer that one can gain a sense of the extension's original condition only from a helicopter.

   Arrows in Figure 38 show the surviving fragments of the retaining walls at the outer edge of the oratory terrace. A three-dimensional reconstruction and plan based on the plane-table survey and aerial photographs are shown in Figures 39 and 40. If the conjectural reconstruction of the retaining wall is accurate, there was barely space for the oratory. So tight was the fit that the retaining wall must have formed the eastern wall of the oratory itself.

The Retaining Wall

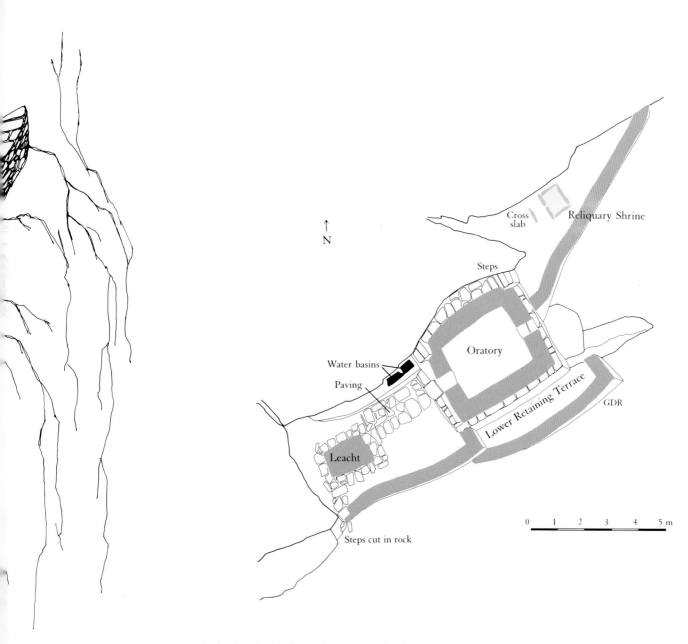

Cross slab

Reliquary Shrine

↑ N

Steps

Oratory

Water basins

Paving

Lower Retaining Terrace

GDR

Leacht

0  1  2  3  4  5 m

Steps cut in rock

Retaining walls had to be built on this terrace before any other construction could take place. The remaining fragments of masonry suggest that two walls were necessary on the southern side, related in a complex manner to the layers of sloping bedrock beneath them. The lower, outer wall brought up the level of the terrace to provide a firm foundation for the south wall of the oratory. At the southeastern corner, where the retaining wall turns in toward the eastern extension, it must have been at least 2.5 meters high. Walls built on precariously inclined surfaces were common in the construction on Skellig Michael. Striking parallels are found, for example, in the retaining wall supporting the terrace of the small oratory of the monastery of Skellig Michael (see Fig. 33). Like the South Peak oratory, this sanctuary was built at the upper end of a surface that falls steeply away. To create a level terrace here required the construction of a retaining wall that reached a maximum height of seven meters. This wall has survived, but until repairs were made on it in 1986, its state was so perilous that it threatened momentarily to collapse.

FIG. 39. *Opposite:* Skellig Michael, South Peak. Conjectural reconstruction of the oratory terrace by Grellan Rourke, based on the plane-table survey of 1986.

FIG. 40. *Above:* Skellig Michael, South Peak. Conjectural plan of the oratory terrace by Grellan Rourke, based on the plane-table survey of 1986.

FIG. 41. *Right:* Skellig Michael, South Peak. Oratory terrace. The vertical slabs, or orthostats, on the eastern extension of the terrace, possibly the remains of a reliquary shrine. Photograph by Jenny White Marshall.

FIG. 42. *Far right:* Island of Illaunloughan in Portmagee channel, County Kerry. An A-shaped reliquary shrine formed by slabs. Drawing by Grellan Rourke.

FIG. 43. *Opposite:* Skellig Michael, South Peak. Aerial view of the summit and the traverse immediately below it. The final rock face to be scaled on the way to the summit rises from this traverse. The dotted line shows the route to the traverse and the outer terrace. Photograph taken in 1987 by Con Brogan. Courtesy Office of Public Works.

## The Eastern Extension of the Oratory Terrace

15. The total area of the terrace extension is 10.5 square meters.

16. The first stone is .45 meter long, .35 meter high, and .15 meter thick; the stone at right angles to it measures .65 meter long, .35 meter high, and .05 meter thick. The third orthostat, located to the west of the other two, is .6 meter long, .25 meter high, and .1 meter thick.

17. County Kerry has five extant above-ground examples of such shrines: at Caherbarnagh, Illaunloughan, Killabuonia, Killoluaig, and Kilpecan. See Henry, 1957; Thomas, 1971, 142, 143. Fanning, 1981, and O'Kelly, 1958, found, after excavating at Church Island and Reask, the remnants of two others. Thomas comments that four of the extant examples of reliquary shrines in Kerry are set within rectangular enclosures formed by vertically set stone slabs.

The eastern extension of the terrace measures roughly 7 by 3 meters (see Figs. 29 and 32). A narrow triangular-shaped space, it slopes steeply to both the south and the east and was originally joined to the principal terrace by a wall.[15] The extension is clearly part of the original plan for the terrace, an integral part of its construction. The labor required to create even a small amount of usable space suggests that this extension served some fundamental, important purpose.

Three stone slabs on the extension furnish a clue to this purpose. Two of them stand at right angles to each other; the third lies somewhat west of the other two (Fig. 41).[16] These upright slabs, or orthostats, were very likely part of a rectangular reliquary shrine constructed of stone slabs. The relics of holy men were venerated in Ireland, as in the rest of the Christian world during this period, although the manner in which the relics were contained and displayed varied according to local custom. In Kerry outdoor reliquary shrines may still be seen on several ecclesiastical sites, such as the island of Illaunloughan, in the Portmagee channel (Fig. 42).[17] Here, as in other known examples, the shrine is constructed of stone slabs set to form an A-shaped structure. Rectangular reliquary shrines formed by upright slabs are unknown. But at the monastery of Skellig Michael orthostats were used to form rectangular frames for the graveyard and for a *leacht*.

The creation of a separate place for a reliquary shrine makes sense if we consider the small area of the oratory terrace, but spatial separation may also reflect a symbolic significance. The area surrounding several of the Kerry slab shrines was marked off by small rectangular enclosures, a tangible reminder that the shrines were sacred.

Could a reliquary shrine have been constructed here to venerate a holy monk who had used the South Peak as a place of temporary retreat before the hermitage was built? It is easy to imagine that the arduous struggles of such an extraordinary monk might have inspired the construction of the South Peak hermitage.

From the oratory terrace the climber doubles back to the trail that leads to the summit, an unusually wide and long dry-stone masonry traverse, 9 by 2 meters (Fig. 43), that ends at the foot of the last perpendicular rock face. On the way up to this traverse one views with amazement a fragment of dry-stone wall built by someone who must have been kneeling on clouds when he placed these stones on a narrow ledge that plummets into what appears to be eternity (Fig. 44). Early in our investigations we believed that this wall once formed part of a beehive cell, the dwelling of the hermit (see the discussion on pages 59–65).

The long traverse is falling away at the point where one must rely on it in beginning the final ascent. Once more the climber faces the now-familiar routine of reaching for handholds and footholds up a vertical defile before gaining the safety of a narrow ledge of solid rock just below the summit.

FROM THE ORATORY TERRACE TO THE SUMMIT

The summit is small—a few rock ledges—and consists of the ultimate peak of the rock, crowned by a modern iron weathervane, and the Spit. Smith (1756, 115) noted that pilgrims called the summit "the eagle's nest, probably from its extreme height; for here, a person seems to have got into the superior region of the air." The Spit, a narrow ridge some two meters below the weathervane on the eastern side of the peak, was legendary (Fig. 45). At its far end lay the goal of the pilgrims—the upright slab that had to be kissed. Most writers on the South Peak, from Smith in 1756 to Hayward in 1946, mentioned the slab. Sometime after 1977, however, it disappeared, probably falling from its base. No part has ever been found, and only traces of dry-stone masonry remain in the socket where the slab had been anchored by layered stone. Fortunately, archaeologists made photographs and took measurements of the

FIG. 44. *Opposite:* Skellig Michael, South Peak. Retaining wall forming the corner of the outer terrace, viewed from the ascent from the oratory terrace to the traverse shown in Figure 43. Photograph by Walter Horn.

FIG. 45. *Above:* Skellig Michael, South Peak. Aerial view from the south, showing the placement of the Spit. Photograph by Walter Horn. (See Fig. 13 for a comprehensive view showing the same placement.)

FIG. 46. *Above:* Skellig Michael, South Peak. Photograph taken by Des Lavelle in 1976, showing the upright slab still standing then at the easternmost end of the Spit.

FIG. 47. *Opposite:* Skellig Michael, South Peak. Photograph taken by Paddy O'Leary in 1977, showing the upright slab that once stood at the easternmost end of the Spit.

18. We are grateful to Des Lavelle and Paddy O'Leary for permitting us to use their photographs. After the disappearance of the slab in 1977, Des Lavelle searched for it not only in Christ's Saddle below but on the ocean floor, in sea diving expeditions.

slab in 1977 (Figs. 46, 47).[18] The visible part of the slab was approximately 1 meter high and 7.6 centimeters thick. No design was engraved on it, but a tiny cross, barely perceptible, was scratched into the surface, perhaps by a pilgrim.

The Spit itself is roughly 3 meters long and varies in width, narrowing in the middle to only .2 meter. It is reached from a lower rock to its west, and it can be partly circumnavigated at its base on a campion-covered ledge. The Spit projects over the jagged valley hundreds of feet below. Stepping upon it is chilling; more commonly people sit and inch along its narrow downward-sloping surface.

There are no archaeological vestiges on the summit that we can relate with certainty to the hermitage. Although the slab at the end of the Spit may have been placed there by a hermit, it may also have been erected later by zealous pilgrims. The summit was surely important to the hermitage nonetheless, for to gain access to the outer terrace it was necessary first to climb almost to the summit.

THE OUTER TERRACE

The isolation of the outer terrace relative to the other terraces of the hermitage, as well as its distance from them, shows clearly in Figure 43 (see also Figs. 12 and 13). Even the contour of this terrace is odd, making it the most awkward of the man-made terraces to photograph and to describe. There is no one spot or angle on the rock from which it can be viewed in its entirety; only an aerial view shows its contours (Figs. 48, 49).

FIG. 48. Skellig Michael, South Peak. Aerial view of the outer terrace taken from the northern side of the peak. A short stretch of the lighthouse road is visible at upper left as well as some of the monastic stairways connecting this road with Christ's Saddle. Arrows (from left) mark the Spit; the rock mass below which, on the other side of the peak, the oratory terrace is located (see Fig. 45); the garden terrace; (below) the outer terrace; and the Needle's Eye. Photograph by Walter Horn.

Essentially this area that we refer to as a terrace is structurally dissimilar to the others on the South Peak, for the masonry remains here consist of only a seventeen-meter-long wall along the perimeter. Nor are there signs that a single unified platform supported by retaining walls was ever intended. The construction of such a level terrace would be nearly impossible, for the topography consists of three natural stepped ledges whose elevations differ by as much as four meters. The terrain is irregular and steep, containing only a few square meters of level ground; moreover, there is no defining boundary on the northern and eastern sides.

The terrace is not mentioned in the accounts of earlier explorers, except for a casual remark of Lord Dunraven's: "There are also curious portions of an ancient wall on certain projections of rock near the Spit" (see p. 18). Liam de Paor also noted "some faint and somewhat doubtful traces of construction at one or two points along the way" (see p. 18). We believe that these remarks refer either to the small rounded section of wall visible on the climb

FIG. 50. Skellig Michael, South Peak. Part of the difficult path to the corner of the outer terrace. The corner lies at the outer edge of a projecting spur of rock on the southwestern side of the South Peak some six meters below the summit. Photograph by Walter Horn.

to the traverse below the summit (see Fig. 44) or to a larger section of wall visible from the summit itself (Fig. 50; the wall begins at about the level of the traverse and is lost to sight at the rounded section). These two small sections are all that can be seen of the outer terrace without climbing down to it.

The constant powerful winds blowing across the exposed terrain of the area below the summit make access to the outer terrace treacherous. No path exists, so one must climb gingerly down rough, sharp-edged ridges to reach the point where the masonry wall begins. Here one walks down along the top of the wall, perhaps planned at this point as a walkway, to reach a rock outcropping on which a few footholds have been carved. The footholds lead to level ground just where the wall turns a corner, where originally we believed a dry-stone beehive cell was located.

The first reaction is to gasp at the daring construction, to marvel at the stunning Atlantic beauty of the site, and to wonder, Why? Why was this ever built, this wall hanging on the edge of space? The first hermit who left

FIG. 51. Skellig Michael, South Peak. Outer terrace. A detail of the corner, clearly revealing what looks like corbeled stonework. Photograph by Walter Horn.

the monastery was going in one direction only—up, closer to God through a life of complete isolation on the island's highest point. Yet to inhabit this desolate area without shelter from winter storms was impossible. Could the outer terrace have been the location of the hermit's living quarters? Our first response to this question was an intuitive no. How could anyone survive on this storm- and rain-lashed ledge, where a freakish gust of wind might cause a loss of footing and a fatal fall? Because we could find no traces of a shelter on the lower man-made terraces on the peak, however, the question persisted. If the outer terrace were not the site of the hermit's dwelling, what was the purpose of its bizarre and extensive masonry? The construction of the wall, carefully built of medium-sized building stones with good internal and external faces, required intensive labor in an inhospitable, barely accessible area. What imperturbable man (or men) would carry building materials over a considerable distance to set stone upon stone on ledges that leave no room for even a stumble? As one contemplates this construction, one wonders whether at some point devotional submissiveness might have shifted imperceptibly into devotional hubris.

Although we know that construction is itself unequivocal evidence that the terrace was important, even as we continued our explorations we were unable to resolve our questions about the use of this site. On the most prominent part of the outer terrace, the corner, a curved and apparently corbeled wall looks like the surviving portion of a cell (Fig. 51). Further investigation showed, however, that instead of curving inward to form a small cell, the walls spread outward to follow topographical contours. Moreover, when the stones that had fallen into the interior were removed, what had looked like corbeling was revealed to be only a few courses high; the courses had been constructed so that the projecting rock became part of the wall, which elsewhere has a vertical face. Therefore it is not possible that a corbeled cell was constructed here, even though this may well have been the location of some sort of shelter.

This corner offers the best place on the outer terrace to construct an effective protection from the wind and weather, particularly because the ground level is one meter below that of the surrounding terrain. The argument for the presence of a shelter was strengthened by the discovery of a few pieces of rough flagging at the base of the corner. Had the entire area been flagged, there would have been a space just large enough for a recumbent hermit. Although final judgment awaits the clearing away of all the fallen rock, it can nevertheless be stated that an exceptionally minimal sheltered area probably existed here.

At the corner, the external height of the wall is now 2.5 meters, the internal height 1.07 meters, and the width of the wall from .6 to .8 meter at its present level. It is extraordinary that as one looks at the masonry from above, one is unaware that this semicircle of stones forms the top of a wall. Originally this wall was higher, possibly three to four meters high if it connected with the masonry above as indicated by the dotted line on Figure 52.

FIG. 52. Skellig Michael, South Peak. Remains of the walls that form the southeastern boundary of the outer terrace. Photograph by Walter Horn. Dotted line indicates the possible height of the original masonry.

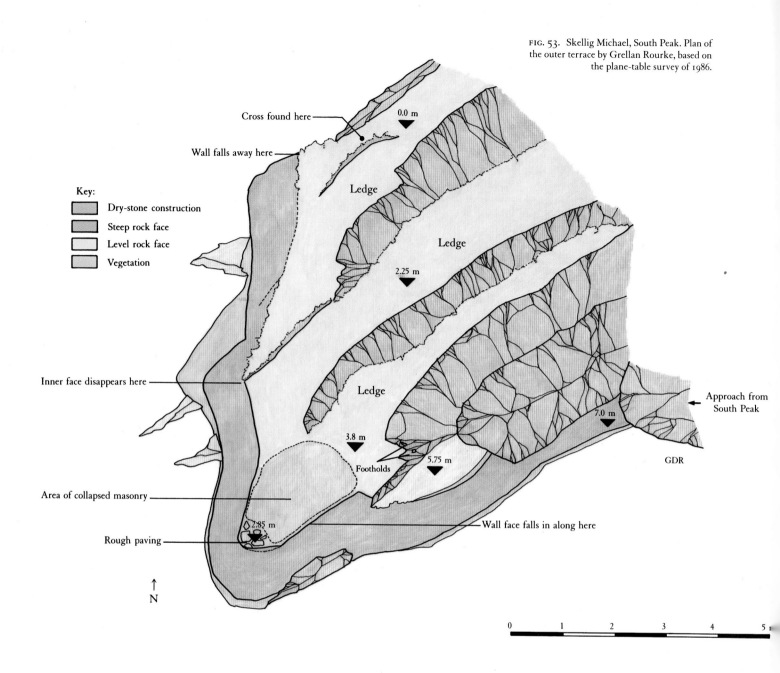

FIG. 53. Skellig Michael, South Peak. Plan of
the outer terrace by Grellan Rourke, based on
the plane-table survey of 1986.

Cross found here

Wall falls away here

Key:

Dry-stone construction
Steep rock face
Level rock face
Vegetation

0.0 m

Ledge

Ledge

2.25 m

Inner face disappears here

Ledge

Approach from
South Peak

7.0 m

3.8 m

GDR

Footholds

5.75 m

Area of collapsed masonry

Wall face falls in along here

2.85 m

Rough paving

↑
N

0    1    2    3    4    5 m

The lowest, northwestern, section of this terrace is even more
puzzling than the corner. Here the wall curves, following an irrational downward course to a level 3.8 meters below the corner. Some seven meters lie
between the highest point of the wall fragments on the south side of the outer
terrace and those on the lowest, northwestern, side (Fig. 53). The external face
of this wall is quite high in two places, about 3.2 meters. The original height
of this wall and the function of the area it enclosed remain a mystery. The
downward-curving wall is too far below the corner to have protected it from
the wind. For this purpose, an inward-curving wall at a higher level, even at
the level of the second ledge, would have been more effective. Perhaps the
lower walls provided some shelter for a prayer station, however, for a small
hand-sized cross, roughly shaped, was found in this area (Figs. 54 and 55).

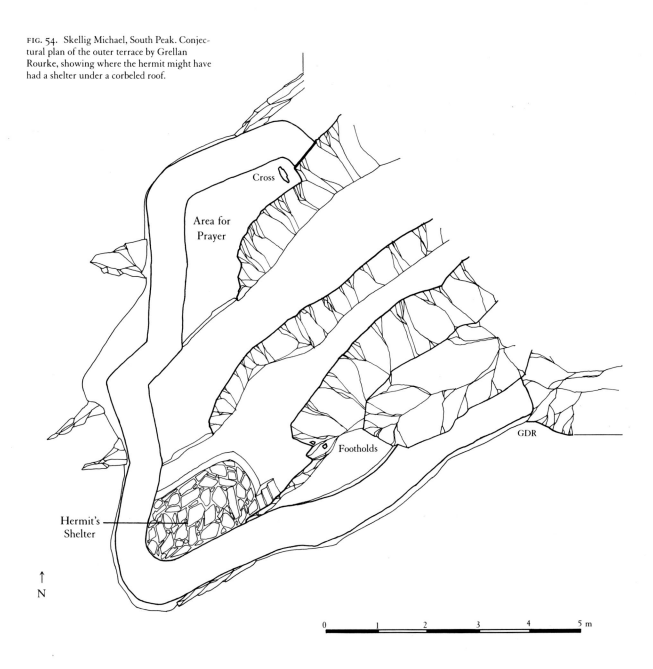

FIG. 54. Skellig Michael, South Peak. Conjectural plan of the outer terrace by Grellan Rourke, showing where the hermit might have had a shelter under a corbeled roof.

Cross

Area for Prayer

GDR

Footholds

Hermit's Shelter

↑
N

0  1  2  3  4  5 m

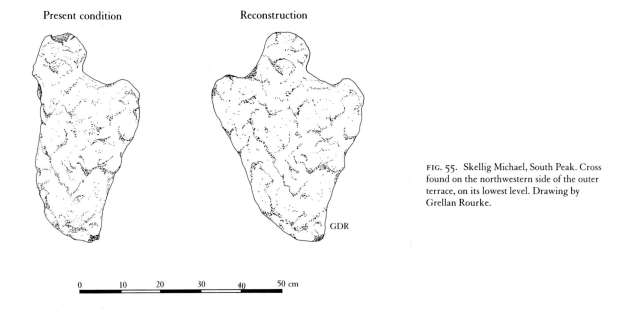

Present condition

Reconstruction

GDR

FIG. 55. Skellig Michael, South Peak. Cross found on the northwestern side of the outer terrace, on its lowest level. Drawing by Grellan Rourke.

0  10  20  30  40  50 cm

19. The climate on the peak where the monastery is located is also determined by a combination of other factors such as solar aspect and the albedo and heat retention capacity of the native bedrock (written communication from R. Berger, professor of geography and chairman, Department of Archaeology, University of California at Los Angeles).
20. It is possible that the better climate existing in the Early Christian period, at its peak in the tenth and twelfth centuries, may have ameliorated conditions somewhat. It is almost impossible, however, to assess the main climatic difference—that there were fewer storms of lessened intensity—for a hermit living on the South Peak.

Even as we speculated about the possibility that a minimal dwelling had been constructed on the outer terrace, we faced an additional question: Could anyone have endured there during severe storms? Even on sunny, warm days the South Peak winds are strong, sometimes dangerous, and this terrace is the one most exposed to wind.

Ocean winds normally sweep horizontally over the surface of the water. When their passage is blocked by the flank of an island such as Skellig Michael, with peaks rising to a considerable height, their force changes from horizontal to vertical. The resulting wind, sweeping upward, does not cease immediately on reaching the highest points of the island but pushes beyond, curving gradually back into its horizontal course under the pressure of the wind that surrounds and follows it. The resulting condition is referred to as a leeward vortex, a comparatively calm zone suspended in turbulent winds. These wind forces are largely responsible for the warmer, calmer microclimate that exists at the location of the monastery.[19]

The effects of the monastery's microclimate were dramatically demonstrated to us when we visited Skellig Michael early in the spring of 1972. The crossing was rough, and all of us were thoroughly chilled, despite our heavy layers of sweaters and our knitted caps. As we landed, the skipper, Dermot Walsh, advised us to leave all heavy clothing below because an entirely different, warmer, climate existed up at the monastery. Although in our chilled state we were reluctant to shed our warm gear, we found the skipper's advice borne out when we reached the summit and were able to discard our heavy clothing.

Could similar illogical climatic variations be expected on the wind-lashed top of the South Peak? The two peaks differ significantly in their conformation and size. The monastery was built at the southern end of an extensive inclined rock plateau that rises some fifteen meters behind it, ensuring the continued upward sweep of the north and west winds past the monastery. The South Peak has a much smaller mass and rises to a greater height than the monastic peak. As it rises, it loses much of its bulk, so that at the level of the outer terrace there is no protection from the wind. A microclimate here similar to that of the monastery summit is impossible. Walls to deflect the wind would be critical for protection on this terrace.[20]

The rock formation and wall provide good protection from southern and southeastern winds. The wall on the northwestern side provides partial protection from winds. No such barrier, however, exists on the northern or northeastern sides of the terrace. There a hermit would have been exposed to the full force of the worst storms coming from those directions.

These barriers interacting could provide only marginal protection on this desolate site in good weather and would be completely inadequate in winter or during a major storm. No one could survive such conditions without better shelter. Moreover, during rainstorms, torrents of water cascading off the ledges guarantee that anyone on the outer terrace will be thoroughly drenched. Winds of near-hurricane force make movement to and from the terraces extremely hazardous, if not impossible. A hermit may have spent many a stormy night praying in the oratory, on the best-protected terrace on the South Peak. Even under the best conditions, however, he would frequently have been cold, wet, and at risk of serious injury or death. But the goal of an ascetic was not comfort; the Cambray Homily reminds us:

> This is our denial of ourselves, if we do not indulge our desires and if we abjure our sins. This is our taking-up of our cross upon us, if we receive loss and martyrdom and suffering for Christ's sake.[21]

21. "Ocuis numsechethse . isée ar n-diltuth dúnn fanissin mani cometsam de ar tolaib ocuis ma fristossam de ar pecthib. issí ticsál ar cruche dúnn furnn ma arfóimam dammint ocus martri ocus coicsath ar Chriist" (Cambray Homily in *Thesaurus Paleohibernicus,* ed. and trans. Stokes and Strachan [1901], 1975, 2:245).

# IV :: THE ENIGMA OF THE HERMIT'S DWELLING

*I wish, O son of the Living God,*

*ancient eternal King, for a secret hut in*

*the wilderness that it may be*

*my dwelling.*

Anonymous Irish poem, ninth century

As we began our investigations, we had a well-formulated view of the nature of the three terraces and believed that the three major components of a hermitage—an oratory, a dwelling, and a garden—had, for lack of space, been neatly separated so that each terrace would sustain one element. At the end of several summers of on-site examination, however, we reluctantly concluded that only on the oratory terrace was there any evidence supporting this ordered concept. The scale of the construction, the presence of the oratory, and the discovery of the water basins all establish that this terrace was a clearly definable part of a permanent hermitage. We are particularly troubled and puzzled, therefore, that we could find no uncontestable evidence of a dwelling anywhere on the peak. A protected dwelling was essential for survival on the exposed ledges of the South Peak, but where was it?

The oratory, the most important building of a hermitage, had to be built on a ledge where it could be oriented with the altar at the east, the arrangement of all Christian churches in the Early Christian period. The safest and best-protected ledge, therefore, was used for the oratory rather than for a dwelling. Because there was not enough room on the oratory terrace for a hermit's dwelling as well, the only other possible locations were the outer terrace and the garden terrace.

The evidence for a dwelling in the corner of the outer terrace has already been discussed (see pp. 59–65). A severely ascetic shelter may have existed in this outer area, removed from the other two terraces. To live there, however, would have required extraordinary fervor—even for a Skellig monk. The rude shelter that could have been built there would have been inadequate for a hermit living on the peak. Nor would the topography permit the construction of a cell elsewhere on the outer terrace.

The other possible location for a dwelling, the garden terrace, is in many ways as enigmatic as the outer terrace because the evidence remaining offers no proof at all about its use. Nevertheless, a sizable dry-stone terrace was created there, one that was not necessary to the ascent. We have already discussed our reasons for conjecturing that this terrace was used as a garden (see pp. 36–37); it is possible, however, that in addition to this use, this terrace served as the site of a dwelling.

Logically, the garden terrace was the optimal place for a small cell: it was close to and connected with the oratory terrace. Moreover, there was enough level space to build a cell at the point where the garden terrace broadens to almost five meters.[1] But this broadest point is precisely where time and weather have eroded much of the fill—and with it any trace of the foundations or walls of such a structure.[2] Figure 56 shows a conjectural cell sited on the terrace; it is well protected, with its entrance, like those of the cells in the monastery, oriented to the south. This cell would have provided an internal floorspace of 2.3 by 1.7 meters. A dwelling here would help to explain why two passages link the oratory and garden terraces—one over the hump, the other around the outer edge of the rock between them—and would offer a compelling motivation for the construction of the terrace itself.[3]

But a dwelling and the shadow cast by it would have reduced the amount of space available for a garden by roughly half, thereby considerably diminishing its ability to meet even the simple needs of a hermit. Was this a garden terrace without a dwelling or a dwelling terrace with a small garden? We have not been able to come to a consensus of opinion on this matter.

1. The only extant trace of a wall on this terrace consists of a curve 1.3 meters long, made of small stones, that is located on top of the retaining wall. Although in itself it is inconclusive, it is located in the widest section of the terrace, the only place suited to building a structure.

2. Almost one-third of the fill has disappeared from the garden terrace. Dwellings in the Early Christian period were customarily built without deep foundations; however, Rourke has calculated that even a foundation about .4 meter below the original ground level would be higher than the present level of the terrace.

3. Horn disagrees with his coauthors, supporting his own view as follows: There is no doubt that the hermit was in need of a garden, and it cannot be questioned that the garden terrace was the only place on the peak that could have served that function. But if the surface area of this terrace was reduced by the space required for the construction of a beehive hut, the terrace would no longer have been large enough to accommodate the needs of a hermit. The garden terraces of the monastery of Skellig Michael give us the means of calculating with a high degree of accuracy the amount of garden space needed per monk in a community of its size. In the monastery garden 540 square meters were available for planting. If, as the sleeping space available in the beehive huts and the traditions of Early Christian monasteries in Ireland suggest, twelve monks and an abbot lived at the monastery, then 41.5 square meters per monk were available for planting at the monastery of Skellig Michael. In contrast, the entire area available for cultivation on the garden terrace was 17.5 square meters. A beehive hut at the center of the terrace would have reduced this area to 9 square meters— far too little to supply the needs of a hermit. It is possible, moreover, that the hermit used the oratory as his dwelling, as I believe may have been the custom with small churches such as Tech Molaise (*tech,* "house" or "habitation") on the island of Inishmurray, County Sligo. In this church is a bench that the islanders call the Saint's Bed (Wakeman 1886, 213–23).

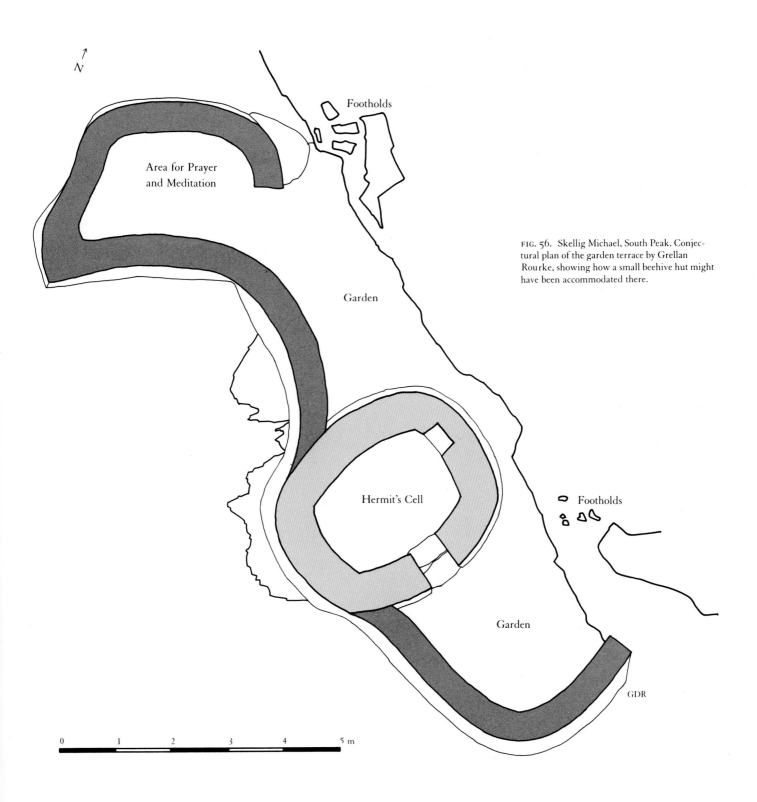

N

Footholds

Area for Prayer
and Meditation

Garden

FIG. 56. Skellig Michael, South Peak. Conjectural plan of the garden terrace by Grellan Rourke, showing how a small beehive hut might have been accommodated there.

Hermit's Cell

Footholds

Garden

GDR

0   1   2   3   4   5 m

V :: THE DATE OF THE HERMITAGE

We believe that the South Peak hermitage was most likely built sometime in the ninth century. No unequivocal evidence supports this contention; rather it is based on circumstantial evidence, some of it archaeological, some cultural.

The style of unmortared wall construction used in the man-made terraces and buildings of the hermitage is identical to that of the unmortared oratories and dwellings of the monastery of Skellig Michael. This masonry style, found in many west coast island monasteries, is typical of the Early Christian period in Ireland. Thus although architectural comparison suggests that the monastery and the hermitage were both built in this period, it does not reveal which was built first. There are, however, good reasons for assuming that the construction of the monastery preceded that of the hermitage.

If a hermitage had been established on Great Skellig before the founding of the monastery, there would have been no need to seek out the South Peak to find isolation. A retreat could have been built on what became the monastic summit, which is more readily accessible and climatically suitable. But once a monastery had been founded, the only place of retreat left on the island for a man who desired to come closer to God was an even higher and less accessible spot, the South Peak.

There is a more compelling functional reason for believing that the hermitage was constructed after the monastery. The monk who secluded himself from the monastery undoubtedly had the full approval of his brothers, for he needed their spiritual and, more important, their physical support. One man alone could not have built the South Peak hermitage. This was no simple rustic retreat of wattle and daub, idyllically situated in a forest near a stream—it was nothing like the conveniently located, easily built hermitage so movingly described in a poem from the seventh-century life of St. Déglán of the Déisi:

> For he was in his own dear cell which he had built himself, for himself. It is between wood and water in a strait and secret spot on the sea's brink, and a clear stream flows by it from the wood to the sea, and trees gird it beautifully round about; and this is called the little desert of Declan [Déglán].[1]

ARCHAEOLOGICAL EVIDENCE

1. For the Latin version of the *Vita Sancti Declani* see *Vitae Sanctorum Hiberniae,* ed. Plummer, 1910, 2:32–59. The passage quoted here is on p. 58. The Gaelic version, edited and translated by Patrick Power from a manuscript in the Bibliothèque Royale in Brussels, was published in 1914 in Irish Texts Society 16, 2–72, under the title *Life of St. Declan of Ardmore and Life of St. Machuda of Lismore* (passage here quoted is on pp. 68–69).

The South Peak hermitage had nothing in common with Déglán's. Situated out in the Atlantic, it lacked easily available food supplies, water, and shelter. Far from being simply composed, it consisted of massive masonry structures and substantial dry-stone terraces for steady passage between stages of the ascent, and it had extraordinary, far-reaching retaining walls in addition to an oratory and a dwelling. All this construction took a prodigious amount of work. To carry and lay the stones was a monumental task, particularly since the only access to the building site was a tortuous scramble through a rock chimney and up almost sheer cliff faces. The scale of the work required a stable and flourishing base of operations, which means that the monastery had to have been well established before the hermitage could be started. The complexity and scale of construction also indicate that the monastery planned to use the hermitage over a long period of time.

The construction of a hermitage by a monastery has specific historical precedents. The Venerable Bede describes the building of St. Cuthbert's hermitage on Farne Island as follows:

> And when he had expelled these hostile forces, the brethren helped him to build a tiny dwelling surrounded with a ditch, and such essential buildings as an oratory and a communal shelter. He then directed the brethren to dig a well in the floor of the shelter, although the ground was hard and stony and there seemed no hope whatever of finding a spring.[2]

2. Bede, *A History of the English Church and People,* trans. Sherley-Price, 1955, 261. A "communal shelter" was one for domestic use.

Another reason to believe that the hermitage could have been built only by a well-established monastery is the need for workers with experience and specialized building skills. The monastery furnished the model for solving the problems posed by building on Skellig Michael, since the only possible site for a monastery was the huge shelf of bedrock slanting seaward from the top of the northeastern peak at an angle of almost forty-five-degrees. In this setting, retaining walls were a topographical sine qua non for the level terraces of the monastery gardens and for the level spaces that accommodated the oratories and beehive cells. No other monastery in Ireland was built on such difficult terrain; Skellig Michael is absolutely unique in this respect. Without the knowledge and experience gained in this construction, the South Peak hermitage, with its more difficult and dangerous terrain, would have been impossible to build (Fig. 57).

Materials to construct the hermitage were available because weathering—largely the effect of frost along the island's major fault and cleavage lines—had broken down the rock, producing large quantities of loose stone and friable zones of easily quarried surface rock. No evidence exists for large-scale quarrying on the South Peak, but some small-scale quarrying occurred. The most important quarrying site was the oratory terrace, where about four cubic meters were taken from the area above the water basins. Moreover, there was a small amount of quarrying on the north side of the peak and on the outer terrace. The remaining building materials must have been gathered either from loose stone lying on the peak's ledges or from Christ's Saddle, where stone is readily available.[3] Generally, the stone was unworked, although some that was used for wall faces was roughly squared off. Much of the fill material used to create the terraces is not indigenous to the South Peak. Tons of it must have been carried up or lifted by rope through the Needle's Eye in leather bags.[4]

Constructing the platforms and terraces of the hermitage was an exceptionally dangerous undertaking. The manipulation of heavy slabs of stone into position as a secure base for retaining walls was an arduous and formidable task, particularly on the oratory terrace. Stout ropes to secure the laboring monks would have been necessary on the perilous slopes. The work must have proceeded at a slow pace and would have required nerves of steel. The monks' achievement is a mark of their great determination, skill, and spiritual zeal.

Other, historical, considerations enable us to attain a higher degree of probability in dating the hermitage than archaeological evidence permits: the great ascetic revival of the ninth century, the possible effect of the ninth-century Viking raids on the Skellig monks, and the dating of the cross slab found on the oratory terrace.

HISTORICAL CONSIDERATIONS

3. Moreover, Michael O'Sullivan does not believe that the shape of the garden terrace is an altogether natural one and suggests that a certain amount of quarrying was done to level it and expand its width. He notes that he "would expect weathering to reflect the subtle bedding contrast we have here [i.e., between fine sandstone and siltstone] and to produce only a slight indentation on the rock face at bed boundaries—this is not the case here; the terrace 'cut' displays a pronounced bench feature. The cleavage plane orientation would not promote the development of such a rebate as the site is oriented 'across the grain', and I would expect the rear wall to be a jointplane, rather than a hackly surface" (written communication, March 1, 1988).

4. O'Sullivan, 1987. In a written communication in 1988, he noted further that some quarrying may well have been carried out below the Needle's Eye, pointing out the availability of accessible fractured rock in a bedding surface near the lowest steps cut into the rock just above Christ's Saddle. A complete investigation of all the quarrying sites has not been attempted.

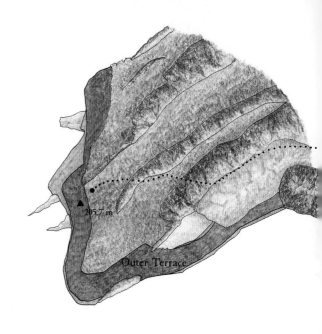

Outer Terrace

205.7 m

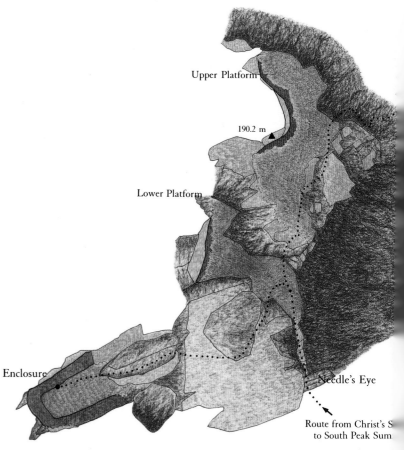

Upper Platform

190.2 m

Lower Platform

Enclosure

Needle's Eye

Route from Christ's S
to South Peak Sum

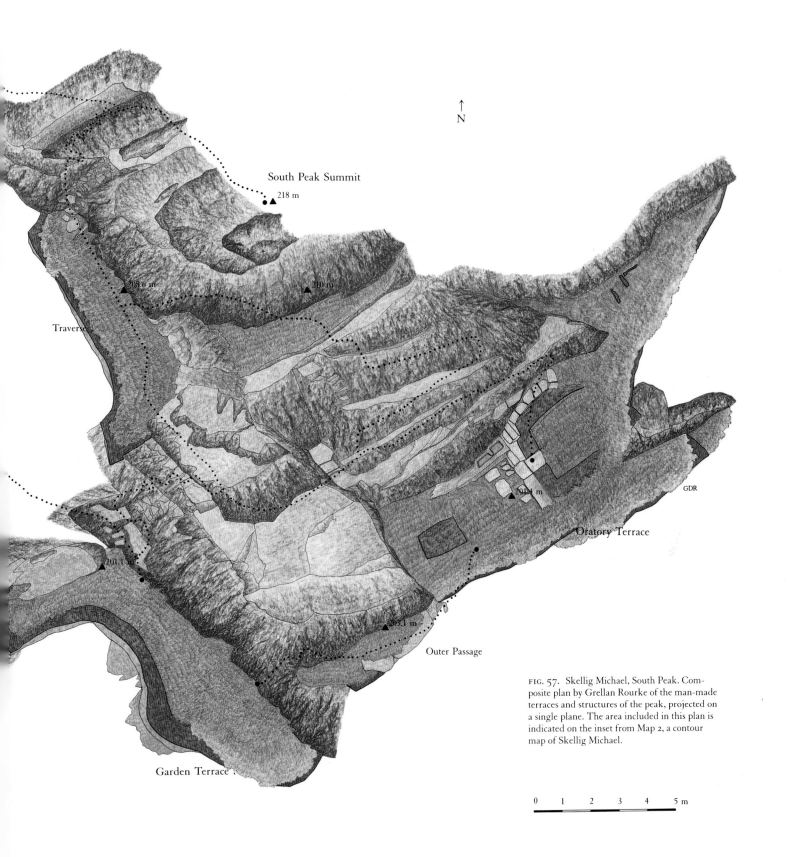

North arrow:
↑
N

South Peak Summit
218 m

208.6 m
210 m

Traverse

201.1 m

201.4 m

GDR

Oratory Terrace

203.1 m

Outer Passage

FIG. 57. Skellig Michael, South Peak. Composite plan by Grellan Rourke of the man-made terraces and structures of the peak, projected on a single plane. The area included in this plan is indicated on the inset from Map 2, a contour map of Skellig Michael.

Garden Terrace

0   1   2   3   4   5 m

## The Ascetic Revival of the Ninth Century

Ascetic solitaries were common in the Irish church at a very early date. The ascetic tradition of the sixth and seventh centuries was particularly strong and remained so until the eighth century, when it suffered a temporary decline with the growth and secularization of the great monastic *paruchiae*. The ascetic revival of the late eighth and early ninth centuries was led by a group of highly articulate and persuasive monks who referred to themselves as the Célí Dé, the "companions of God," but were popularly referred to as the Culdees. We are convinced that the hermitage of the South Peak is an expression of Skellig Michael's enthusiasm for the Culdee revival. To understand the cultural and chronological implications of this movement we must review briefly the history of Irish eremitism and the fluctuating attitudes of the Irish toward the anchoritic ideal during the first few centuries after monasticism was introduced into Ireland.

One of the outstanding characteristics of Irish monasticism was the desire to imitate as closely as possible the monastic pattern of the first desert monks of Egypt. The life of the solitary ascetic who fled the world in search of union with God was celebrated in Europe, as in Egypt, as the highest and purest form of monastic life. St. Anthony, whose life and deeds in the Thebaid desert had been a major force in popularizing monasticism in the fourth century, was the heroic exemplar. The biography of St. Anthony by Athanasius (ca. 296–377) helped to disseminate Antonian asceticism throughout Europe.[5] In St. Martin (ca. 316–400) Europe found its counterpart to St. Anthony, and soon the *Life of St. Martin* by Sulpicius Severus (ca. 363–420) circulated throughout Europe along with the *Life of Anthony*.[6] Solitary asceticism was praised throughout Europe, but nowhere was it imitated so faithfully, for so long, or on such a grand scale as in Ireland. Enthusiastically adopting Antonian ideals, early Irish monks began with hermitages and small eremitic colonies. The sixth-century Irish monk Columbanus exhorted his fellows: "Let us die to ourselves that we may live to Christ; for we cannot live to Him unless first we die to ourselves, that is, to our wills."[7] In another sermon he admonished his followers, "Have no mercy on transitory things, lest you lose what is eternal; the whole world is foreign to you who are born and buried bare."[8] Thus two centuries and a continent away, the words and spirit were still entirely Antonian.

In adhering to this spirit, the Irish monks constantly sought the equivalent of the Egyptian desert. On the Irish mainland the locations of old hermitages are still recognizable by the name *dysert* or *disert*. The most determined ascetics, however, sought their desert on islands in the sea. The hagiographies contain countless references to monks searching for "a solitude in the pathless sea."[9]

The second half of the sixth century saw the beginning of another aspect of Irish monachism: the creation of monastic *paruchiae*. These were monastic communities, geographically widespread but united in confederation under the rule of the abbot of the chief monastery. This organizational structure was directly related to the preexisting secular social system in which several petty kings owed allegiance to an overking; in fact, *paruchiae* were

5. St. Athanasius wrote his *Vita Antonii* shortly after the death (356/357) of the great anchorite to furnish monks in other parts of the world with a model of ascetic life and to reassure the church that monachism was not heretical but orthodox. In 388 the treatise was translated into Latin by Evagrius of Antioch. For a translation into English with a rich body of textual annotations, see Athanasius, *The Life of Antony and the Letter to Marcellinus*, trans. Gregg, 1980.
6. For a recent edition of the Latin text translated into French by Jacques Fontaine, see the Bibliography under Sulpicius Severus. A translation into English by Alexander Roberts can be found under the same heading.
7. "Nosque nobis moriamur ut Christo vivamus; ei enim vivere non possumus nisi nobis ante, hoc est, nostris voluntatibus moriamur" (*Sancti Columbani Opera*, ed. and trans. Walker, 1957, 102–3).
8. "Ne parcas caducis, ne aeterna perdas; alienus tibi totus mundus est, qui nudus natus nudus sepeliris" (ibid., 78–79).
9. The *Vita Sancti Columbae* by Adamnan is full of these references. The following example is typical: "Some of our brethren have lately set sail, and are anxious to discover a desert in the pathless sea." (Aliqui ex nostris nuper emigraverunt, desertum in pelago intransmeabili invenire optantes) (ed. and trans. Reeves, 1874, 71, 185).

frequently allied with and supported by the ruling families. For example, all of the monasteries belonging to the *paruchia* of St. Columba were in the territory controlled by his family, the Uí Néill, and seven of the first eight abbots of Iona, the chief Columban monastery, were relatives of St. Columba's. In time, economic and social dependence on aristocratic families caused the gradual secularization of many of the great monastic confederations.[10]

During the seventh century monastic *paruchiae* were becoming increasingly important and common. But the earlier Egyptian ideals of ascetic simplicity and austerity were not forgotten, and monasteries continued to support and encourage ascetics. It was not unusual for the founders of monasteries to spend some time as hermits, either early in life or upon the approach of old age.[11] The great scholastic monastery of Bangor still consciously looked to the model of Egyptian monachism and felt itself the direct spiritual descendant of Egypt. The *Antiphonary of Bangor,* written between 680 and 691, makes some nineteen references to Egypt; the attitude embodied in them is summed up perfectly in one of the quatrains:

> A House full of Delights
> Built on Rock
> A veritable vine
> Transmitted from Egypt.

> Domus deliciis plena
> Super petram constructa
> Necon vinea vera
> Ex Aegypto transducta.[12]

By the eighth century the monastic *paruchiae* exercised effective control over the Irish church. The great wealth and power resulting from their alliance with ruling families led to the creation of great monastic schools from which beautiful manuscripts and decorative metalwork emerged. Inevitably in a system where family lands were frequently also monastic lands and where the monastic and the secular were often inseparable and indistinguishable from each other, a certain secularization of the monasteries occurred. In some cases abbacies became secular and administrative, and their succession passed down not only in families but also from father to son. Abbot Corman of the Monasterboice monastery died in 764 and was succeeded by his son Dub-da-inber. At Trevet between 774 and 839 a father, son, and grandson made up the abbatial succession. This increasing secularization of monasteries, though not inherently evil, did facilitate abuses of monastic ideals. The difference was blurred between goals, attitudes, and position in the spiritual and secular worlds.[13]

Monks even went to war. In 764 Clonmacnoise and Durrow were involved in an armed conflict in which two hundred men of Durrow are said to have been killed. In Emain Macha in 759 Ulstermen fought with the southern Uí Néill. According to *The Annals of Tigernach* this battle took place "at

10. For a discussion of the formation of *paruchiae,* see de Paor and de Paor [1958], 1967, 50–51; Hughes [1966], 1980, chap. 7.

11. St. Cuthbert spent most of the last eleven years of his life in a hermitage on Farne Island after retiring as abbot of Lindisfarne in 676. St. Fursey spent some time as a hermit on an island in Lough Corrib near Galway (ca. 630) before he traveled to England and the Continent to found monasteries (Henry 1963, 1:41). On Fursey see also Bede, trans. Sherley-Price, 1955, bk. 3, chap. 19.

12. For the text see *Antiphonary of Bangor,* ed. Warren, 1895, 2:28. The date is discussed in the introduction to that volume.

13. For a lucid account of the secularization of the church in the eighth century, see Hughes [1966], 1980, 163.

the will of Airechtach, priest of Armagh through discord with Abbot Fer-dá-chrich" (Hughes [1966] 1980, 170). The references to ecclesiastical synods, common in the sixth and seventh centuries, declined in the eighth century, suggesting that the abbots were looking more to the secular kings than to their fellow churchmen for support (Hughes [1966] 1980, 170–72).

By the late eighth century a reaction to this state of affairs resulted in a great Irish ascetic and anchoritic revival. The reformers were determined to remove from monachism any preoccupation with secular affairs; in general they sought a return to the old desert ideal of prayer, meditation, and asceticism (Hughes [1966] 1980, 173–77). The most influential leader of this movement was Máel-ruain, founder of the monastery of Tallaght, a community of ascetics. His followers, unlike earlier ascetics, were forbidden to go on pilgrimage and were instructed to avoid worldly disputes and to avoid asking visitors for news of the world, "since it might harass and disturb the mind of him to whom it was told."[14]

In addition to forming communities of ascetics, individual Culdees commonly attached themselves as anchorites to one of the great monasteries. In two manuscripts dating from the period 830–840 a monk has recorded the customs and discipline of Máel-ruain and his chief disciple Máel-díthruib of Terryglass, making several references to this practice. "A certain anchorite lived in Clonmacnoise named Laisren, quite naked and free from sin"; and "there was a certain anchorite from Slain—Now he had dairying and store of victuals given him by the monastery."[15]

The Culdees were not the only practitioners of this anchoritic revival. The ninth-century Rule of Columba advised hermits to be by themselves in a retired spot near a chief monastery. The monastery could provide food, clothes, and spiritual direction; the anchorite, in turn, could spend part of his day teaching, writing, or otherwise assisting the monastery. In the ninth century the term *anchorite* meant a monk who practiced severe asceticism. He could be a solitary recluse or the chief scribe of a monastery who went into seclusion for only part of the year. The chief duties of the ascetic were prayer and study. But if a monk could not bring himself to tears of compunction in his prayers, the Rule counseled him to turn to manual labor until he sweat (1873, 119, 121).

By example and word, Culdees became the most important ascetic force in Ireland during the late eighth and ninth centuries. Their beliefs spread in part because of the fame of their scholarship. The two main Culdee monasteries, Tallaght and Findglais, were called the two eyes of Ireland in a ninth-century monastic text, *The Triads of Ireland*.[16] From these monasteries came several manuscripts containing the Culdee doctrine: the *Monastery of Tallaght*, the *Teaching of Máel-ruain*, and the *Rule of the Célí Dé*. Additionally, there is a section on Culdees in the ninth-century work the *Rule of St. Carthage*.[17]

Yet powerful as was the Culdees' influence during this period, it did nothing to alter the basic organizational structure of the Irish church. Lack of uniformity was one outstanding characteristic of the early Irish mo-

14. "Indtí *tra* dotháod día accaldim som ni fogni laisim fachmarc scel dóib acht atorbai *fr*isa tíagad ambai*n*. Fobíthin fobenad ⁊ doairmescad me*n*mai*n* iond caich día naisnedtar" (*Monastery of Tallaght*, ed. and trans. Gwynn and Purton, 1911, 127–28; cf. Hughes [1966], 1980, 176).
15. "Araile ancarae robui hi cluaoin mac naois laisrien a ainm imnocht imdilmain cen ní for a cubus" (*Monastery of Tallaght*, 155). "Báoi alaile anchoire antuaid o sláne colcu. Coibnius dochuttae. Rochachti iarum commor corroabstinit. Robaoi iarum áirgi laisim o muindtir taiseit on muindtir" (159).
16. "Di snil Herenn-Tamlachta, Findglais," *The Triads of Ireland*, ed. and trans. Meyer, 1906, 3. See also Flower, 1932, 66–75, for a fuller discussion of the role of anchorites and Culdees in ninth-century Ireland. The most complete discussion of the Culdees to date, incorporating all documentary references to them, is found in O'Dwyer, 1981.
17. *The Teaching of Máel-ruain* and *The Rule of the Célí Dé* can be found in *The Rule of Tallaght*, ed. and trans. Gwynn, in *Hermathena* no. 44, 2d supp. vol., 1927, 1–87. The part of the Rule of St. Carthage that discusses the Culdees may be found in Mac-Ewen, 1915, 1:131.

nastic orders; each house had its own rules and practices. There was never any attempt to exercise or enforce the organizational discipline common to continental Benedictines.[18] Following the Culdees' lead was always purely voluntary, a matter of conscience; their appeal to the individual was emotional and carried with it no authority for enforcement. Paradoxically, this may mean that the appeal and influence of the Culdees were greatest among monks, like those of Skellig Michael, who were already living a severely ascetic life.

Spiritual power unsupported by a unified organization tends to dissipate in time. So it was with the influence of the Culdees. The secularization and growth of the great monastic *paruchiae* continued and increased in the tenth century.

The monks of Skellig Michael might have had another reason for their strong interest in supporting the dreams and aspirations of a hermit. In the ninth century the Vikings began to raid the island. After a first bitter experience, in which the monastery was brutalized, the monks would have wanted to build a temporary place of safety from attack.

The earliest undisputed reference to Viking raids on Skellig Michael is in the *Annals of Inisfallen,* where under the year 824 it is stated: "Scelec was plundered by the heathens and Etgal was carried off into captivity, and he died of hunger on their hands."[19] The annals do not tell why Etgal was taken away, but the reason is easy to guess. The Vikings believed that every monastery possessed either valuable objects of gold and silver or important men, like the abbot, who could either be held for ransom or enslaved.

Two mentions of Viking raids appear in the *War of the Gaedhil with the Gaill,* the first in an entry of 821–823 about Etgal, the second (which is undated) after the Etgal entry and before another dated 850:

> There came a fleet from Luimnech in the south of Erinn, they plundered Skellig Michael, and Inishfallen and Disert Donnain and Cluain Mor, and they killed Rudgaile, son of Selbach, the anchorite. It was he whom the angel set loose twice, and the foreigners bound him twice each time.[20]

The monks of Skellig Michael had reason to be anxious, for the approaches to their monastery were not easily defended. The monastery itself could be reached by flights of steps on three sides of the island, on slopes that, apart from steepness, offered no obstacle to armed men. But the hermitage on the South Peak was a different matter. The only access, on the southwest face, was by a single obscure and easily defended passage, the Needle's Eye. This was an insurmountable barrier, where Viking intruders trying to hoist themselves up could easily have been knocked down one by one by a single defender, whom the intruders could not even see. If by chance a hell-bent Viking managed to survive the Needle's Eye, he would still have had to pass three more places from which a monk throwing stones could send him into a headlong plunge.

18. For a discussion of the difference between Irish and Benedictine monachism and a detailed analysis of the organizational philosophy that governed the latter, see the chapter entitled "The Monastic Polity," in Horn and Born, 1979, 327–55. In this same work (vi) readers will find a map showing the origins and diffusion of these two great monastic movements.

19. A.D. 824: "Scelec do orgain do gentib ٦ Etgal do brith i mbrait co n-erbailt gorta léo" (*Annals of Inisfallen,* ed. and trans. MacAirt [1951], 1977, 124–25). The raid is also mentioned under the years 821–823 in the *Annals of Ulster* and the *War of the Gaedhil with the Gaill,* with almost identical wording. References to an earlier raid alleged to have occurred in 812 appear to be untrustworthy. They are based on a manuscript erroneously labeled Annals of Inisfallen. For further information about this academic snarl, see MacAirt's introduction to *Annals of Inisfallen.*

20. "Tanic longes o Luimniuch i ndescert ṅhErend, cor inriset Sceleg Michil, ocus Inis Fathlind, ocus Disirt Donnain, ocus Cluain mor; co ro marbsat Rudgaile mac Trebthaidhi, ocus Cormac mac Selbaig anchora. Is desside ra hoslaic angel po di, ocus poscenglaitis na Gaill cac nuairi" (*War of the Gaedhil with the Gaill,* ed. Todd, 1867, 228–29).

21. *St. Gall Priscian,* margin gloss. Contained in *Thesaurus Palaeohibernicus,* ed. and trans. Stokes and Strachan [1901], 1975, 2:290. For the English version quoted here see de Paor, 1967, 93, n. 2. Another translation, more literal and considerably less poetic, has been published by Stokes and Strachan, 2:290: "Bitter is the wind tonight. It tosses the ocean's white hair: I fear not the coursing of a clear sea by the fierce heroes from Lothlend."

The hermitage was a secure refuge for short periods of time if the monks had sufficient warning. When the ocean was whipped by storms and clouds darkened the skies, the monks felt secure from Viking attack. A poem in the margin of a ninth-century Irish manuscript expresses this feeling with striking beauty. It might well have been written on Skellig Michael.

> The wind is rough tonight
> tossing the white combed ocean.
> I need not dread fierce Vikings
> crossing the Irish Sea.

> Is acher ingaith innocht
> fufuasan fairggae findfolt
> ni agor reimm mora minn
> dondlaechraid lainn ua
> lothlind.[21]

On a clear, calm day, however, the monks could not feel safe, for then maritime attack was a continual threat. To have time to hide their ecclesiastical treasures and flee to safety, the monks needed warning. The hermit on the South Peak was in an excellent position to spot danger and alert the monastery, for from the top he had a 360-degree view of the ocean. No Viking fleet could approach the island unobserved.

## The Date of the Cross Slab

The design on the cross slab found on the hermit's oratory terrace in 1982 is a further means of dating the hermitage. The remains of this cross slab were found under a shallow overgrowth of sea campion approximately one meter west of the hermit's oratory. The left edge, as one faces the cross, is intact and appears to have been shaped, being smooth and straight for most of its length. The right edge is damaged; at its base, the slab is preserved to almost its full original width, but from there upward the edge curves severely inward; and at its clearly broken upper end, the width of the slab is reduced by almost half. Most of the upper part of the engraved design is missing; from the dimensions of the remaining design it can be inferred that in its original state the slab must have been a little over one meter high (Figs. 58 and 59).

This cross belongs to the category known as a developed ring cross—an encircled cross whose arms extend beyond the circle. It is one of the most popular designs for crosses in Ireland and is so closely identified with the Irish that it has become known as the Celtic cross. (For further discussion of the origin and stylistic development of the ring cross, see the Appendix.)

In 1961 Pádraig Lionard studied the use of designs on recumbent cross slabs and was able to develop a typology and chronology for many of them. Outline ring crosses were a popular motif on recumbent slabs, having been engraved on 150 out of 800 to 900 slabs. Two-thirds of the slabs engraved with ring crosses also have inscriptions on them referring to known abbots, ecclesiastics, and princes, thus permitting more precise dating than for most cross designs. The earliest datable example (Fig. 60)—and the only one from

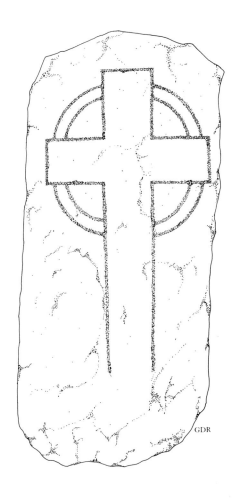

GDR

FIG. 58. *Above left:* Fragment of a slab engraved with a cross, found on the oratory terrace in the summer of 1982. It is 68 centimeters high and 43 centimeters at its widest point. It broke, doubtless, because it is only 1.5 centimeters thick. Photograph by Lee Snodgrass.

FIG. 59. *Above:* Reconstruction of the developed ring cross shown in Figure 58. Drawing by Grellan Rourke.

FIG. 60. *Left:* Clonmacnoise, Offaly. Cross slab decorated with the earliest developed ring cross of Ireland now known. From *Féilscríbhinn Torna,* ed. Séamus Pender.

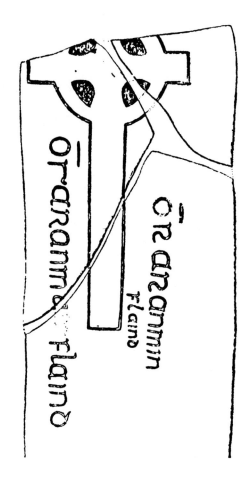

FIG. 61. *Above left:* Fuerte, Roscommon. Cross slab engraved with a developed ring cross and the name Dubinre, probably from the year 814. From Pádraig Lionard, "Early Irish Cross-Slabs."

FIG. 62. *Above:* Iona, Scotland. Cross slab engraved with a developed ring cross and the inscription "Or Ar Anmin Flaind," commemorating Flann, abbot of Iona, d. 891. From Pádraig Lionard, "Early Irish Cross-Slabs."

the eighth century—is on a recumbent slab at Clonmacnoise, inscribed "Or Ar Chuindless," which dates to 720–724 (Lionard 1961, 126). Only one example, moreover, has been dated to the tenth century and none at all to the eleventh. All the others were dated to the ninth century. Two of these are shown in Figures 61 and 62, one from the year 814, the other from 891.

Thus we could date the South Peak hermitage to the ninth century with complete assurance, except that the slab on the South Peak is not recumbent but erect. Lionard notes that the use of outline ring crosses on pillars and erect slabs is uncommon, there being only about fifteen of them.[22] Recumbent grave slabs are always burial markers, whereas small erect slabs were used both for gravestones and for other purposes. Nevertheless, the difference between these small stone markers used in ecclesiastical settings is probably not significant. Indeed, they are so similar that it is frequently hard to differentiate them. Because the design for recumbent slabs was at the height of its popularity during the ninth century, it is highly probable that the few outline ring crosses seen on pillars and erect slabs also belong to this period.

In thus calculating the date of the hermitage, we are aware that we have moved into an area of historical speculation. No individual part of our argument is susceptible to incontrovertible proof. Yet we believe that the argument as a whole carries a high degree of historical persuasiveness.

22. Lionard also notes: "By contrast only 12 of the 26 linear ringed crosses are on recumbent slabs. The main incidence of this latter type is along the west coast where ringed outline crosses are few" (1961, 127). This is the type of detail that gives archaeologists gray hairs.

# VI :: THE FORGOTTEN HERMITAGE

*What they undertook to do*

*they brought to pass;*

*All things hang like a drop of dew*

*Upon a blade of grass.*

W. B. Yeats, "Gratitude to the Unknown
Instructors"

One striking characteristic of this tiny hermitage is that it was invisible from lower levels of the peak and island. From any vantage point in the hermitage, moreover, only parts of the terraces were ever visible to a hermit himself; no overall view was possible. And from below or from the monastery, only the outer retaining walls of the oratory terrace would have been faintly visible. The hermitage, however, was not meant to be seen by men but by God alone. This was a retreat for a monk who found a moderate rule too loose and sought a harder path, like the desert father who "rose, and spread out his hands to heaven, and his fingers shone like ten candles, and [he] said: 'If you will, you could become a living flame'" (*Western Asceticism,* 1958, 57).

After the departure of the Skellig Michael monks, the hermitage was forgotten. By the seventeenth century no memory of it remained. Barely visible from its beginnings, it must have been easy to forget as time passed and the structures began to disintegrate. No details, not even legends, survive about this forgotten place.

Today the only tangible evidence of this extraordinary monastic achievement consists of pieces of crumbling masonry, but the feeling of intense spirituality is still strong in this place. To step out on the Spit and look at the drifting clouds, the heaving ocean below, and birds sailing above is to become deeply conscious of the primeval forces ruling the world. If one stands there on a summer evening as the sea mist rolls in over Little Skellig (Fig. 63), thoughts of the winter misery and hardships of life on the South Peak give way to wonder at the beauty of the scene. Something of the religious joy the hermit felt becomes clear, for surely the hermits of the South Peak shared the belief of another ninth-century anchorite (trans. Flower 1973, 34), who wrote:

> In Tuaim Inbhir I find
> No great house such as mortals build,
> A hermitage that fits my mind
> With sun and moon and starlight filled.

FIG. 63. Little Skellig enveloped in sea mist. Photograph taken from the monastery at 10:00 P.M. in June 1977. Photograph by Walter Horn.

# APPENDIX :: ON THE ORIGIN

# OF THE CELTIC CROSS

*A New Interpretation*

*by Walter Horn*

Developed ring crosses have been universally believed to derive from a simplified, condensed version of the encircled Roman Christogram.[1] Figure 64 shows a typical example from a Romano-British house in Lullingstone, Kent. The design consists of the first two letters of Christ's name in Greek, X (*Chi*) and P (*Rho*), encircled by a triumphal wreath.[2]

By the early fifth century in Europe the Chi-Rho had been simplified from a six-armed figure into something resembling a Latin cross with a P-shaped curl on the upper shaft. The fifth-century sarcophagus of Bishop Theodore in Ravenna displays both the original type and the new, simplified, version, both still surrounded by a wreath. In western Britain by the fifth century the design had been further simplified by substituting a simple circle (or two concentric circles) for the floral motifs of encircling wreaths. This simplification is exemplified in a slab cross from Kirkmadrine in the Rinns of Galloway, diocese of Whithorn (Fig. 65).[3] Finally, the Chi-Rho was converted into a simple cross with equal arms, a Greek cross, as exemplified on the tombstone of an Irish king called Voteporix, who died in the province of Demetia, in southwest Wales, around 550 (Fig. 66).[4] In this form the condensed Chi-Rho was used throughout the Christian world as an important sign of consecration and blessing. In Ireland it was widely diffused and is seen on the Ardagh chalice and in the Book of Durrow.

The developed Irish ring cross is a later phenomenon. The Chi-Rho with arms of equal length (as in Figs. 64 and 65) is replaced by a Latin cross that is too tall to be enclosed by a circle. Instead, the ring forms an integral part of the composition, stabilizing the relation of shaft to transom (see Figs. 60–62). The earliest developed Irish ring cross now known, according to Pádraig Lionard, to whom we owe the most recent and most authoritative study of this subject, is to be found, as I have already mentioned (see pp. 80–83), on a cross slab of Clonmacnoise (see Fig. 60) inscribed "Or Ar Chuindless," that is, "Pray for Chuindless," the abbot of Clonmacnoise attested for the years A.D. 720–724 (Lionard 1961, 126).

A cross slab with a developed ring cross from the Old Church of Kirkinriola, County Antrim, had been assigned to the first half of the seventh century by such scholars as H. C. Lawler and Seán Ó'Ríordáin, who identified the name Degen, to whom this slab is dedicated, with that of a North Irish Bishop Degan or Dagan, who was active in 605 and died in 639 (Lawler 1940, 26; Ó'Ríordáin 1947, 112). Lionard rejects this identification (in a footnote

1. Irish experts hold this opinion, most notable among them Pádraig Lionard, 1961, 95–169.
2. This scheme in turn is descended from the Roman *imago clipeata,* the shield portrait surrounded by a laurel wreath that a triumphant Roman general would hang from his vexillum, or trophy standard. The Christogram was adopted by Constantine in the fourth century as his trophy standard and thereafter became popular throughout Christendom (Roe 1965, 217–18).
3. Thomas, *Early Christian Archaeology,* 1971, dates this slab cross before 500 (107, Fig. 48).
4. Ibid., 110, Fig. 50.

FIG. 64. Lullingstone, Kent. Fresco from a Roman villa. Photograph courtesy of the British
Museum. The Christogram encircled by a triumphal wreath is the Romano-Christian model
for simple Celtic ringed crosses.

only; 127, n. 3) without giving any reasons—but his skepticism, even unex-
plained, is easy to share, for there is not the slightest evidence anywhere in
Ireland (or in the related Celtic territories of England, for that matter) that
would support the assumption that the developed ring cross existed there
as early as the seventh century. This type of cross made its appearance in
the eighth century, but even then appears to have been relatively rare. In the
ninth century it reached an almost unbelievable popularity that stopped with
an uncompromising suddenness by the end of the century.

Conditions in the monastery of Clonmacnoise suggest the ubiquity
of the developed ring cross in ninth-century Ireland. In his study of the grave
slabs of this monastery, Stewart Macalister describes and reproduces no fewer

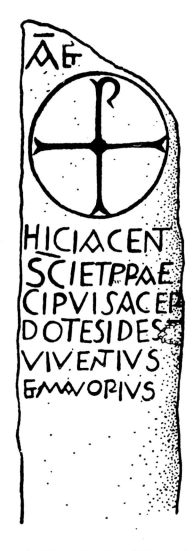

FIG. 65. Kirkmadrine, Rinns of Galloway, diocese of Whithorn. Cross slab, probably late fifth century. Its vertical stem still shows the loop of the P of the Christogram from its Romano-Christian model. From Charles Thomas, *The Early Christian Archaeology of North Britain*.

FIG. 66. Tombstone of Voteporix. Above the king's name an equal-armed cross is enclosed in a ring formed by two concentric circles. From Charles Thomas, *Britain and Ireland in Early Christian Times*, A.D. 400–800.

than 112 of them with the ring-cross design. He points out that this entire body of Celtic crosses must be assigned to the years between 800 and 880 (Macalister 1909, 106). This is only a part, but a significant part, of the total story. "Only one true ringed cross," Lionard tells us, "is dated to the tenth century," and "there is no evidence for a survival into the eleventh century" (127).

Students of Celtic iconography have believed that the transformation of the ring cross with equal arms into the developed ring cross was an autochthonous Irish development.[5] I had no reason to question this belief until the summer of 1984 when during an incidental visit to the Minneapolis Institute of Arts, I was startled to find a Coptic burial shroud of wool and linen that

5. For a superb analysis of the traditional Irish view, see Ó'Ríordáin, 1947, 108–14.

FIG. 67. Coptic burial pall, fifth to seventh century. 138.4 by 68.9 cm. The linen and wool fabric is embroidered with a developed ring cross, a design that became common on Irish cross slabs and high crosses in the eighth and ninth centuries. The vertical shaft terminates in a tongue that rests in a groove in the base, a joint characteristic of timber architecture but not used in stone construction. Photograph courtesy The Minneapolis Institute of Arts.

6. This shroud has been discussed by Lotus Stack, curator of textiles, the Minneapolis Institute of Arts, in *Bulletin de Liaison du Centre Internationale d'Etude des Textiles Anciens*, 1984. An extended version of the same essay is being published in a delayed issue of the *Minneapolis Institute of Arts Bulletin* 66 (1983–1985).
7. Mango, 1962, Figs. 42, 44, 45, and 93. For the date of the mosaics, see Mango, 93–101.

the museum's catalogue assigned to the fifth to seventh century (Fig. 67).[6] The cross shown in this textile is so strikingly similar in design to Irish ring crosses of the eighth and ninth centuries that it is difficult to preclude a developmental interconnection.

Embroidered on the Minneapolis shroud is the image of a large Latin cross with a wreath attached to its arms. The embroidery clearly represents a wooden cross, for its shaft has a tongue at the lower end, which rests in a deep groove made for it in the base. Such tongue-and-groove joints are typical of wood construction but are not at all characteristic of stone carving. That the cross could be detached from its base suggests that it served two functions, one stationary, the other processional.

When I discussed the Coptic shroud with Lotus Stack, the curator of textiles at the Minneapolis Institute of Arts, she showed me photographs of the narthex of St. Sophia in which there seem to be representations of developed ring crosses. From modern photographic views it is difficult to determine the exact nature of the original design of the mosaics. Observations made in 1847–1849 by the Fossati brothers, however, seem to confirm the presence of developed ring crosses. After removing the whitewash that had been applied over the mosaics of the narthex when the church was converted into a mosque, the Fossati brothers made drawings of what they discovered (Fig. 68). The mosaics they brought to light in this manner date from the ninth century, as Cyril Mango has shown.[7]

I must stress that I have not been able to discover any convincing evidence of developed ring crosses at St. Sophia that antedate the ninth century. The sixth-century mosaics in the soffit of the narthex, discussed in volume 1 of Thomas Whittemore's *Mosaics of St. Sophia at Istanbul,* show beautiful examples of Latin crosses forming part of the original sixth-century mosaics of the church (one of these is shown in Fig. 69) but not a single ring cross (Whittemore 1933, Pls. 5, 7, 9, 11).

In a fascinating study entitled "Origins of the Free-standing Stone Cross in Ireland: Imitation or Innovation?" (1987), Nancy Edwards looks at the literary sources attesting the distribution of freestanding wooden crosses of Latin shape in seventh-century Europe. One of the most startling references she examines is in Adamnan's *De locis sanctis,* where a wooden cross of this shape is said to stand in the place where Christ was baptized: "In eodem sacrosancto loco lignea crux summa infixa est" (In this sacred spot a tall wooden cross is implanted). This text, as Edwards correctly infers, identifies the ultimate Near Eastern prototype of the Latin cross.

Crosses of similar shape, Edwards points out, are mentioned in Adamnan's *Life of Columba,* written in 688–692, and in Bede's *Ecclesiastical History.* All of these texts, which she cites word for word, demonstrate that wooden crosses of Latin shape that could be either stuck into the ground or carried were common in seventh-century Ireland and in the Celtic territories along the nearby coast of England. But in Byzantium, as Whittemore has shown, they appear as early as the sixth century (Fig. 69). Thus we must con-

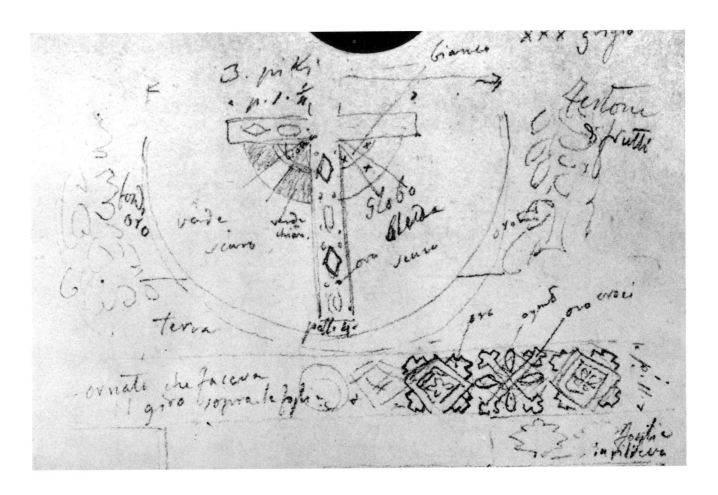

FIG. 68. *Above:* St. Sophia, Istanbul. Developed ring cross in the mosaics of the narthex. Ninth century. Drawn by the Fossati brothers. From Cyril Mango, *Materials for the Study of the Mosaics of St. Sophia at Istanbul.*

FIG. 69. *Left:* St. Sophia, Istanbul. A mosaic from the original sixth-century decoration of the narthex of the church, located in the soffit of bay C of the south cross. From Thomas Whittemore, *The Mosaics of St. Sophia at Istanbul.*

tend with the possibility that the phenomenal spread of the Latin cross in seventh-century Ireland and Celtic England likewise received its primary impetus from the Near East.

It is worth mentioning in this context that of the seven crosses of Latin shape reproduced by Charles Thomas in his *Early Christian Archaeology of North Britain* (1971, Pls. 3 and 4 and Figs. 54, 59, 81, 93, and 98), none seems to antedate the seventh century. In his "Genesis of the Celtic Cross" Seán Ó'Ríordáin expressed the view that the Irish high crosses, which can be dated to the eighth and ninth centuries, are *skeuomorphs* translating into stone the developed ring-cross design embodied in identical crosses fashioned in wood.[8] He based this contention on the depiction of such a cross in a relief on the famous North Cross of Ahenny (Fig. 70) and on the recumbent cross slab of Clonmacnoise (see Fig. 60). The relief at Ahenny shows two priests leading a procession in which a decapitated warrior is being carried home on his horse. One priest holds a crozier; the other carries a ring cross set on a long handle (Fig. 71). The apparent ease with which he carries this cross strongly suggests that it was fashioned of wood.

The recumbent cross slab of Clonmacnoise shows a cross of almost identical design, the foot of which ends in a point—another unmistakable sign of wood construction. Ó'Ríordáin, in his discussion of these monuments, draws attention to the striking architectural parallels of this translation into stone of motifs originally conceived in wood: the curved stone finials of many early Irish churches, which imitate in stone the crossing of the decorated extremities of the gable barge boards of timbered churches.

Unquestionably, both the widespread popularity of ring crosses and their monumentalization into the great high crosses are uniquely Irish phenomena. But it cannot be said with the same assurance that the conversion of the simple ring cross into the developed ring cross is an autochthonous Irish development.

The design on the Coptic textile in the Minneapolis Institute of Arts compels us to conclude that the shape of the developed ring cross as well as the custom of carrying crosses fashioned in this manner in religious processions was influenced by new stimuli from Egypt that reached the Celtic territories of Ireland and England in the eighth century.

FIG. 70. *Opposite:* Ahenny, County Tipperary. High cross (the so-called North Cross), generally assigned to the eighth century on the basis of geometrical motifs and interlacing spirals comparable to those in the Book of Kells. Photograph by Walter Horn.

FIG. 71. *Above:* Ahenny, County Tipperary. High cross (the so-called North Cross). A relief on the east side of the base of the cross. Drawing from Françoise Henry, *Irish High Crosses;* in her *L'Art Irlandais* there is a photograph of this carving.

8. Ó'Ríordáin, 1947, 108–14. W. G. Collingwood, in his study *Northumbrian Crosses of the Pre-Norman Age,* 1927 (5–9, 11, 137), postulated a wooden model for the English high crosses of stone; cf. Champneys, 1910, 75, 215.

FIG. 72. *Right:* Woven ankh, an age-old Egyptian symbol for life, displayed at the State Pushkin Museum of Fine Arts in Moscow, assigned by Shurinova to the fourth century. From Shurinova, *Coptic Textiles in the State Pushkin Museum of Fine Arts, Moscow.*

FIG. 73. *Far right:* Coptic stela from Edfu, now in the British Museum (B.M. 1520), where it is assigned to the fifth to eighth century A.D. It shows an elaborate version of the ankh. From Badawy, *Coptic Art and Archaeology.*

9. The Latin term for this symbol, *crux ansata,* means "cross on a handle"; the obligatory form of this handle was a circle, supported by a cross. On the history of the ankh in Egypt from pharaonic through Early Christian times, see Maria Cramer, 1955.

10. In Badawy, 1978, 215, this stela is dated "A.D. V–VIII." Another example of the same design, from Fayum, is now in the Staatliche Museum of Berlin (see Badawy, 212, where it is dated "A.D. VI–VII."

11. Fig. 74 is from a drawing reproduced by Badawy, 1978, 85, on the basis of a study by Jean Clédat entitled "Fouilles à Khirbet el Flousiyeh." This study is so poorly cited that it is impossible to establish whether it is an article or a book. I did not find it referred to in any library catalogue under the name Jean Clédat and could not trace it in any other way.

Future studies devoted to this problem will have to face an intriguing question: Is the developed ring cross of the Minneapolis shroud a historical descendant of one of the most ancient and ubiquitous Egyptian symbols, the ankh (Fig. 72)? [9] In Early Christian times this symbol was incorporated into such stunning designs as the carving of a stela from Edfu (Fig. 73), consisting of a large Latin cross that carries on its shaft a beautifully tiered and richly ornamented circular enclosure whose diameter is as wide as the transom of the cross beneath it. [10]

My first intuitive response to the question was a clear-cut no. Nevertheless, in our context it is significant that this symbol for life, the ankh, had been important to Egyptian iconography for over a thousand years before the conquest of Egypt by the Romans.

Another combination of ring and cross to which I would draw attention in this connection is in the mosaic paving of the chancel in the North Basilica of Ostracina, built in the sixth century A.D. (Fig. 74). In the paving a cross with arms of equal length is entirely enclosed in a circle. To transform a design of this kind into a developed ring cross would call for no more than a simple extension of the shaft and transom of the cross beyond the enclosing circle. [11]

This step seems actually to have been taken in a non-Christian Egyptian weaving that Klaus Wessel assigns to the fifth century (Fig. 75). In it the head of a youth whom Wessel identifies as Mithras (1963, 236), wearing a Phrygian cap over a crop of curly hair, occupies the center of a circular enclosure. From this enclosure the four arms of a cross, decorated with lions, extend outward to a rectangular frame. It does not matter that this weaving is not Christian. What matters is that it is Egyptian. Klaus Wessel tells us that it was "im Kunsthandel" when he saw it (236). I have not found it referred to anywhere else, but draw attention to a weaving of similar design and clearly

FIG. 74. *Above left:* Marble encrustation in the floor of the chancel of the North Basilica of Ostracina, built in the sixth century A.D. From Badawy, *Coptic Art and Archaeology.*

FIG. 75. *Above:* Non-Christian Egyptian weaving attributed to the fifth century A.D., showing the head of the Persian God Mithras within a circle superimposed on a cross. From Klaus Wessel, *Koptische Kunst: Die Spätantike in Ägypten.*

FIG. 76. *Left:* Christian Egyptian weaving attributed to the fifth century A.D., showing a running lion within a circle superimposed on a cross. From Shurinova, *Coptic Textiles in the State Pushkin Museum of Fine Arts, Moscow.*

Christian derivation that is in the collection of Coptic textiles of the State Pushkin Museum of Fine Arts in Moscow (Fig. 76). Shurinova (1967) assigns it to the fifth century. It shows a running lion in a circular enclosure that is superimposed on the arms of a cross.

In the Mithraic and the Moscow textiles we come as close to the developed Egyptian ring cross of the Minneapolis shroud as one could possibly expect to come in a preceding stage.

# ILLUSTRATIONS

# BIBLIOGRAPHY

Adamnan, *Vita Sancti Columbae.* Edited and translated with copious notes by
    W. Reeves. Historians of Scotland 6. Edinburgh, 1874.

*Adamnan's Life of Columba,* ed. A. O. Anderson and M. Q. Anderson. Edin-
    burgh: T. Nelson, 1961.

Allen, J. Romilly, "Notes on the Antiquities in Co. Kerry visited by the Royal
    Society of Antiquaries of Ireland and the Cambrian Archaeo-
    logical Association, August, 1891." *Royal Society of Antiquaries of
    Ireland* (1892): 282–84.

Andrews, J. A. *A Paper Landscape: The Ordnance Survey in Nineteenth Cen-
    tury Ireland.* Oxford: Clarendon Press, 1975.

*Annals of Inisfallen.* Edited and translated by Seán MacAirt. 1951. Reprint.
    Dublin: Dublin Institute for Advanced Studies, 1977.

*Annals of the Kingdom of Ireland by the Four Masters, from the Earliest Period to
    the Year 1616.* Edited and translated by John O'Donovan. 3 vols.
    Dublin, 1851.

*Annals of Ulster.* Edited and translated by William M. Hennessy. 2 vols. Dub-
    lin, 1887.

*Antiphonary of Bangor.* Edited by F. E. Warren. Vols. 1 and 2. Henry Brad-
    shaw Society 4 and 10. London, 1893 and 1895.

Athanasius, Saint. *The Life of Antony and the Letter to Marcellinus.* Translated
    by Robert C. Gregg. Classics of Western Spirituality. New York:
    Paulist Press, 1980.

Badawy, Alexander. *Coptic Art and Archaeology: The Art of the Christian Egyp-
    tians from the Late Antique to the Middle Ages.* Cambridge: MIT
    Press, 1978.

Bede, the Venerable. *Historiam ecclesiasticam gentis Anglorum Historiam ab-
    batum, Epistolam ad Ecgberctum, una cum Historia abbatum auc-
    tore anonymo, ad fidem codicum manuscriptorum denuo recognovit,
    commentario tam critico quam historico instruxit.* Edited by Carolus
    Plummer. 2 vols. Oxford, 1896.

————. *A History of the English Church and People.* Translated by Leo Sherley-Price. Harmondsworth, England: Penguin, 1955. Revised by R. E. Latham, 1968.

Bernard. *Vita Malachiae.* Translated by H. J. Lawlor, in *St. Bernard of Clairvaux's Life of St. Malachy of Armagh.* Society for Promoting Christian Knowledge. New York, 1920.

*The Book of Leinster* (formerly *Lebar na Núachongbála*). Edited by R. I. Best, O. Bergin and M. A. O'Brien. 5 vols. Dublin: Dublin Institute for Advanced Studies, 1954–1967.

Cabrol, F. and H. Leclerq. *Dictionnaire d'Archéologie et de Liturgie.* 15 vols. Paris, 1903–1953.

*Calendar of Documents Relating to Ireland, 1302–04.* Ed. H. S. Sweetman and G. F. Handcock. Vol. 5, 294–99. London, 1875–1886. Reprint. London: Nendeln, 1974.

Champneys, Arthur C. *Irish Ecclesiastical Architecture.* London: George Bell and Sons, 1910.

Chatterton, Lady. *Rambles in the South of Ireland.* 2 vols. London, 1839.

Collingwood, W. G. *Northumbrian Crosses of the Pre-Norman Age.* London: Faber and Guyer, 1927.

Cramer, Maria. *Das Altägyptische Lebenszeichen im Christlichen (Koptischen) Ägypten.* Eine Kultur- und Religionsgeschichtliche Studie auf Archaologischer Grundlage. Wiesbaden, 1955.

de Paor, Liam. "A Survey of Sceilg Mhichíl." *Journal of the Royal Society of Antiquaries of Ireland* 85 (1955): 174–87.

————. "The Age of the Viking Wars." In *The Course of Irish History,* edited by T. W. Moody and F. X. Martin, 91–106. Cork: Mercier Press, 1967.

de Paor, Máire, and Liam de Paor. *Early Christian Ireland.* 1958. Reprint. London: Thames and Hudson, 1967.

Dunning, P. J. "The Arroasian Order in Medieval Ireland." *Irish Historical Studies* 4 (November 16, 1945): 297–315.

Dunraven, Edwin Richard Windham Wyndham-Quin, Third Earl of Dunraven. *Notes on Irish Architecture,* edited by Margaret Stokes. 2 vols. London: George Bell and Sons, 1875 and 1877.

Edwards, Nancy. "Origins of the Free-standing Cross in Ireland: Imitation or Innovation?" *Bulletin of the Board of Celtic Studies.* Cardiff: University of Wales Press, 1985.

Fanning, Thomas. "Excavation of an Early Christian Cemetery and Settlement at Reask, County Kerry." *Proceedings of the Royal Irish Academy* 81 C (1981): 65–163.

*Féilscríbhinn Torna.* Edited by Séamus Pender. Cork, Ireland: Cork University Press, 1947.

Flower, Robin. "The Two Eyes of Ireland." In *The Church of Ireland,* edited by W. Bell and N. D. Emerson, 66–75. Dublin: Church of Ireland Printing and Publishing Co., 1932.

————. *The Irish Tradition.* 1947. Reprint. London: Oxford University Press, 1973.

Foley, Patrick. *The Ancient and Present State of the Skelligs, Blasket Islands, Donquin, and the West of Dingle.* Dublin, 1903.

Giraldus Cambrensis. *Topographia Hibernica et expugnatio Hibernica.* Edited by J. F. Dimock. Rolls Series 21. Vol. 5 of *Giraldi Cambrensis Opera.* London, 1867.

————. *The History and Topography of Ireland.* Edited and translated by John J. O'Meara. Dundalk, Ireland: Dundalgan Press, 1951. Rev. ed. Harmondsworth, England: Penguin, 1982.

Gogarty, Thomas. "Documents concerning Arch. Dowdall." *Archivium Hibernicum,* vols. 1–2. Dublin: M. H. Gill and Son, 1912–1913.

Gwynn, Aubrey, and R. Nevill Hadcock. *Medieval Religious Houses in Ireland.* Harlow, England: Longman, 1970.

Harbison, Peter. "John Windele's Visit to Skellig Michael in 1851." *Journal of the Kerry Archaeological and Historical Society* (1976): 125–48.

————. "High Crosses." In *Irish Art and Architecture from Prehistory to the Present,* edited by Peter Harbison, Homan Potterton, and Jeanne Sheehy. London: Thames and Hudson, 1978.

102 :: BIBLIOGRAPHY

Hayward, Richard. *In the Kingdom of Kerry.* 1946. Reprint. Dundalk: Dundalgan Press, 1976.

Henry, Françoise. *Irish Art in the Early Christian Period.* 1940. Rev. ed. London: Methuen, 1965.

————. "Early Monasteries, Beehive Huts, and Dry-stone Houses." *Proceedings of the Royal Irish Academy* 58 (1957): 127–79.

————. *L'Art Irlandais.* 3 vols. Paris: Zodiaque Press, 1963.

————. *Irish High Crosses.* Published for the Cultural Relations Committee of Ireland. Dublin: Three Candles, 1964.

Herity, Michael. "The Layout of Irish Early Christian Monasticism." In *Ireland and Europe,* edited by P. Ní Chatháin and M. Richter, 105–16. Stuttgart: Klett-Cotta, 1984.

Horn, Walter. "On the Origins of the Medieval Cloister." *Gesta* 12 (1973): 14–52.

Horn, Walter, and Ernest Born. *The Plan of St. Gall.* 3 vols. Berkeley: University of California Press, 1979.

Hughes, Kathleen. *The Church in Early Irish Society.* London, 1966. Reprint. London: Methuen, 1980.

————. *Early Christian Ireland: Introduction to the Sources.* Sources of History: Studies in the Uses of Historical Evidence 6. London: Hodder and Stoughton, 1972.

Lamb, H. H. *Climate: Present, Past, and Future.* 2 vols. London: Methuen, 1972–1977.

*Landscape Archaeology in Ireland.* Edited by Terence Reeves-Smyth and Fred Hammond. British Archaeological Research, British Series 116, 1983.

Lavelle, Des. *Skellig: Island Outpost of Europe.* Dublin: O'Brien Press, 1977.

Leask, Harold G. *Irish Churches and Monastic Buildings.* 3 vols. Dundalk: Dundalgan Press, 1955.

*Lebor Gabála Érenn.* Edited and translated by R.A.S. Macalister. 5 parts. Irish Texts Society. Dublin, 1938–1956.

*Life of St. Declan of Ardmore and Life of St. Machuda of Lismore.* Edited and translated by Patrick Power. Irish Texts Society 16. London, 1914.

Lionard, Pádraig. "Early Irish Cross-Slabs." Edited by Françoise Henry. *Proceedings of the Royal Irish Academy* 61 C (1961): 95–169.

Macalister, Stewart, R.A. *The Memorial Slabs of Clonmacnois, Kings County, with an Appendix on the Materials for a History of the Monastery.* Dublin, 1909. Printed at the University Press for the Royal Society of Antiquaries of Ireland.

Macaulay, Kenneth. *The Story of St. Kilda.* London, 1764.

MacEwen, Alexander. *A History of the Church in Scotland.* 2 vols. Rev. ed. London and New York: Hodder and Stoughton, 1915.

Maclean, Charles. *Island on the Edge of the World: The Story of St. Kilda.* New York: Taplinger, 1980.

Mango, Cyril. *Materials for the Study of the Mosaics of St. Sophia at Istanbul.* Dumbarton Oaks Studies 8. Washington, D.C.: Dumbarton Oaks Library, 1962.

Martin, Martin. *A Voyage to St. Kilda.* London, 1698; reprinted subsequently many times.

*The Martyrology of Tallaght.* From the *Book of Leinster* and MS 5100-4 in the Royal Library, Brussels, MS 5100-104. Edited by R. I. Best and H. J. Lawlor. London: Harrison and Sons, 1931.

Mason, Thomas H. *The Islands of Ireland.* London: B. T. Batsford, 1936.

Mayer Thurman, Crista C., and Bruce Williams. *Ancient Textiles from Nubia: Meroitic X-Group and Christian Fabrics from Ballane and Oustul.* Exhibition catalogue. Art Institute of Chicago, 1979.

*Monastery of Tallaght.* Edited and translated by E. J. Gwynn and W. J. Purton. *Proceedings of the Royal Irish Academy* 29 (1911): 115–79.

Nicol, Donald M. *Meteora: The Rock Monasteries of Thessaly.* London: Chapman and Hall, 1963.

O'Connor, Thomas. *Ordnance Survey Letters of 1841, Kerry 403 and 405–13.* Dublin: Archives of the National Monuments Service.

O'Dwyer, Peter. *Célí Dé: Spiritual Reform in Ireland, 750–900.* Dublin, 1981.

O'Kelly, Michael J. "Church Island near Valentia, Co. Kerry." *Proceedings of the Royal Irish Academy* 59 C (1958): 57–136.

*Ordnance Survey Map of 1841, Kerry 104.* Dublin: Archives of the National Monuments Service.

Ó'Ríordáin, Seán. "The Genesis of the Celtic Cross." In *Féilscríbhinn Torna,* edited by Séamus Pender, 108–14. Cork, Ireland: Cork University Press, 1947.

O'Sullivan, Friar of Muckross Abbey. "Ancient History of the Kingdom of Kerry." Edited by Fr. Jarlath Prendergast. *Journal of the Cork Historical and Archaeological Society* 4–6 (1898–1900).

O'Sullivan, Michael. "Geological Aspects of the Constructions above the Needle's Eye on the South Peak of Skellig Michael." Report to the Commissioners of National Monuments, 1987.

Pender, Séamus, ed. *Essays and Studies Presented to Professor Tadgh Ua Donnchada (Torna) on the Occasion of His Seventieth Birthday, September 4, 1944.* See *Féilscríbhinn Torna.*

Reeves-Smyth, Terence. "Landscapes in Paper: Cartographic Sources for Irish Archaeology." In *Landscape Archaeology in Ireland,* edited by Terence Reeves-Smyth and Fred Hammond, 119–77. British Archaeological Research, British Series 116, 1983.

Roe, Helen. "The Irish Cross, Morphology and Iconography." *Journal of the Royal Society of Irish Antiquaries* 95 (1965): 213–18.

———. "The Cult of St. Michael in Ireland." In *Folk and Farm,* edited by C. O'Danachair. Dublin: Royal Society of Antiquaries of Ireland, 1976.

*Rule of St. Columba.* Edited and translated by Arthur W. Haddan and William Stubbs. Vol. 2, art. 1, Appendix A. Councils and Ecclesiastical Documents Relating to Great Britain and Ireland. Oxford, 1873.

*The Rule of Tallaght* (containing *The Teaching of Máel-ruain* and *The Rule of the Célí Dé*). Edited and translated by Edward Gwynn. In *Hermathena* no. 44, 2d supp. vol. Dublin: Hodges, Figgis and Co.; London: Longmans, Green and Co., 1927.

*Sancti Columbani Opera.* Edited and translated by G.S.M. Walker. Scriptores Latini Hiberniae 2. Dublin: Dublin Institute for Advanced Studies, 1957.

Severus, Sulpicius. *The Works of Sulpicius Severus.* Translated by Alexander Roberts. Select Library of Nicene and Postnicene Fathers of the Church 11. 1890–1900, 1–122.

———. *Vie de Saint Martin.* Translated by Jacques Fontaine. Sources Chrétiennes 3. Paris: Les Editions du Cerf, 1969.

Shurinova, R. *Coptic Textiles in the State Pushkin Museum of Fine Arts, Moscow* (in Russian, with an illustrated catalogue written both in Russian and English). Moscow, 1967.

Smith, Charles. *The Ancient and Present State of the County of Kerry.* Dublin, 1756. Reprint. Cork: Mercier Press, 1969.

Stack, Lotus. "A Christian Cross—a Woven Representation at the Minneapolis Institute of Arts." *Bulletin de Liaison du Centre Internationale d'Etude des Textiles Anciens* (1984): 59–60.

Stokes, Margaret. *Early Christian Architecture in Ireland.* London, 1878.

*Thesaurus Palaeohibernicus: A Collection of Old-Irish Glosses, Scholia, Prose, and Verse.* Edited and translated by Whitley Stokes and John Strachan. 2 vols. 1901. Reprint. Oxford: Oxford University Press, 1975.

Thomas, Charles. *Britain and Ireland in Early Christian Times,* A.D. *400–800.* London: Thames and Hudson, 1971.

————. *The Early Christian Archaeology of North Britain.* London: Oxford University Press, 1971.

*The Triads of Ireland.* Edited and translated by Kuno Meyer. Royal Irish Academy Todd Lecture Series 13. Dublin, 1906.

*Two Lives of Saint Cuthbert: A Life by an Anonymous Monk of Lindisfarne and Bede's Prose Life.* Edited and translated by Bertram Colgrave. Cambridge: Cambridge University Press, 1940.

*Vitae Sanctorum Hiberniae, Partim Hactenus Ineditae ad Fidem Codicum Manuscriptorum Recognovit Prolegominis Notis Indicibus Instruxit.* Edited by Charles Plummer. 2 vols. Oxford: Clarendon Press, 1910.

Wakeman, W. F. "A Survey of the Antiquarian Remains of the Island of Inishmurray." *The Journal of the Royal Historical and Archaeological Association of Ireland.* Vol. 7, 4th series. Dublin, 1886; rpt. London and Edinburgh, 1893.

Wallace, Patrick F. "A Reappraisal of the Archaeological Significance of Wood Quay." In *Viking Dublin Exposed,* edited by John Bradley. Dublin: O'Brien Press, 1984.

Walsh, Rev. T. J., and Denis O'Sullivan. "St. Malachy, the Gill Abbey of Cork, and the Rule of Arrouaise." *Journal of the Cork Historical and Archaeological Society* 54 (1949): 40–61.

*War of the Gaedhil with the Gaill; or, the Invasion of Ireland by the Danes and Other Norsemen.* Edited by James Henthorn Todd. London, 1867.

Wessel, Klaus. *Koptische Kunst: Die Spätantike in Ägypten.* Recklinghausen, 1963.

*Western Asceticism.* Translated by Owen Chadwick. Library of Christian Classics 12. Philadelphia: Westminster Press, 1958.

Westropp, T. J. "Cruise in Connection with the Munster Meeting, a Descriptive Sketch of Places Visited." *Journal of the Royal Society of Antiquaries of Ireland* 17 (1897): 265–358. (Also included in *The Antiquarian Handbook.* Edited by R. Cochrane. Royal Society of the Academy of Ireland, 1904.)

Whittemore, Thomas. *The Mosaics of St. Sophia at Istanbul.* Preliminary Report on the First Year's Work, 1931–1932. Oxford University Press for the Byzantine Institute, 1933.

Wilson, T. G. *The Irish Lighthouse Service.* Dublin: Allen and Figgis, 1968.

Windele, John. *Journals on Travels in Cork and Kerry, 1826–1851.* Handwritten manuscript in the library of the Royal Irish Academy. MS 12c. 11. (For a valuable, though incomplete, reprint of Windele's text, see Harbison 1976.)

Wyndham-Quin, Edwin Richard Windham. *See* Dunraven.

# INDEX

Note: Italicized page numbers indicate illustrations.

| | |
|---:|:---|
| Designer: | Steve Renick |
| Compositor: | G & S Typesetters, Inc. |
| Text: | Linotron 202 Granjon |
| Display: | Granjon |
| Printer: | Toppan Printing Co., Ltd. |
| Binder: | Toppan Printing Co., Ltd. |
| Editorial Coordinator: | Stephanie Fay |
| Production Coordinator: | Ellen M. Herman |

# DATE DUE